TINKERS, TOWNIES AND TOFFS

Rod Brammer

KBO Authors

Copyright © 2021 Matt Brammer

All rights reserved

The characters and events portrayed in this book are fictitious. Any similarity to real persons, living or dead, is coincidental and not intended by the author.

No part of this book may be reproduced, or stored in a retrieval system, or transmitted in any form or by any means, electronic, mechanical, photocopying, recording, or otherwise, without express written permission of the publisher except for the use of brief quotations in a book review.

CONTENTS

Title Page
Copyright
GLOSSARY
TINKERS, TOWNIES AND TOFFS   1
BEFORE WE START…   2
CHAPTER ONE   3
CHAPTER TWO   6
CHAPTER THREE   11
CHAPTER FOUR   30
CHAPTER FIVE   53
CHAPTER SIX   81
CHAPTER SEVEN   98
CHAPTER EIGHT   127
CHAPTER NINE   137
CHAPTER TEN   148
CHAPTER ELEVEN   163
CHAPTER TWELVE   173
AND NOW WE END…   184
ABOUT THE AUTHOR   185
SHALDEN SHOOTING SCHOOL   187

GLOSSARY

1. Tobey: Foxes are given different names in different parts of the country – in Devon he is 'Charlie', in Surrey 'Charles', in Hampshire 'Tobey'.

2. Peewits = Lapwings = Green Plovers

3. Hares: are called Madam, Puss or Marjory in Hampshire.

4. Hares: run in lots of different ways: bouncing along in long flowing hops, running upright, half speed, flattened out, low and fast to avoid flying predators are just some of them.

5. Leach: wash out in the rain.

6. Mended: a fish is said to be 'mended' if it has fully recovered from spawning and is up to normal weight and colour.

7. Grilse: salmon having been in the sea perhaps a year.

8. Law: weighing things in favour of the hunted, shot or fished for quarry, e.g. Law in hare coursing is giving the hare a long head start before the dogs are slipped.

9. Jug: partridges roost on the ground in small groups, at this time of the year in family groups. They are said to jug, jug down.

10. Plump: a group of wildfowl, ducks, made up probably of several families of the same group.

11.	Skeined: a vee formation of wildfowl. They skein out when they are flying long distances. The most forward of the birds break up the air for those following. They are generally older, stronger fowl and the toughest to eat.

12.	Tobey: foxes are nicknamed Tobey in Hampshire. In some parts of the country they are nicknamed Charlie or Reynard.

13.	Earth: a fox normally lives in a hole in the ground call an earth; a badger lives in a sett and an otter lives in a holt.

14.	Rack: a purpose-made gap between rows of trees, for passage or extraction of timber.

15.	Brashed: branches cut from the bole, cut close to give clear grained timber.

16.	Tramlines: wheel marks left in the crop that match the current tractors and machines on the farm, sprayer, fertiliser. They remain as the crop grows, leaving double lines through the crop, looking like tramcar rails.

17.	Tuberculosis tested and clear.

18.	Coppiced: cut every seven years for a yield of hurdle-making poles, poles for runner beans etc. Woods are coppiced in sequence, the resultant poles are sold through the timber yard.

19.	Stools : the original trees that were planted about one hundred years ago. They are harvested of their layered rods, once every seven years – they reshoot. This is 'sustainable woodland', known about for centuries. The way the pseudo-conservationists go on about it, one would think they had invented coppicing.

20.   Straw ride: an area of barley straw laid on a ride to encourage game birds and song birds to come and feed. They like to scratch about in the straw.

21.   Pre-charged: the best modern air-rifles have a compressed air bottle to throw the pellet. They have no recoil and very little sound; if fitted with a silencer they cannot be heard from ten yards away. They are wonderfully accurate, with no great springs to compress – just the thing for a sporting lady.

22.   Leached out: washed out by rain or artificial watering.

23.   Potato scab: a skin disease on the tubers, caused by wrong seed in the wrong place – too much lime (basic slag has the same effect).

24.   Basic slag: crushed and powder slag from the steel industry, has the same effect as lime, raising the ph and adding trace elements to the soil, very good as a grass dressing.

25.   First early: potatoes are sold as seed in three groups in England, first early – second early – main crop. Self-explanatory really – first early, new potatoes in the shops; second early follow on; the main crop are those which come in September and store over winter.

26.   Clunch: spoil from a chalk quarry, mainly flint, chalk and clay.

27.   Jag: foul hook or snatch the fish with large treble hooks.

28.   Reds: area in the headwaters of a river where salmon lay their eggs.

29.   Fry: a creature recognisable as a young fish, with gills, fins and able to swim.

30. Hand: where the tail joins the body; a salmon may be held here, the actual tail will spread and allow it. Sea trout, sometimes confused with a salmon, cannot be held like this. The tail collapses, and it will slip from your hand.

31. Necked: when the ears bend acutely downwards, cutting off any sap moving. The ears snap off too early if this happens, too early being before the combine can cut the crop.

32. Two and a quarter hundredweights: one hundred and fifteen kilos approx. – for those of my age, about the same as a man weighing 18 stone.

33. Stretchability: make a strong enough dough to rise properly.

34. Hagburg: the scientific name for the stretchability of the dough.

35. Early bite: a crop grown specifically for dairy cows to graze before the grass comes in the spring.

36. Come over the back: grain is said to 'come over the back' if it spills out from the straw discharge. There will always be some – if there is a lot the drum and concave are not set properly or the ground speed is too quick.

37. Claws: the cow has cloven hooves; that is, in two parts. The two separate parts are, colloquially, claws. Between these high up the foot, the foot is soft and vulnerable – a footbath keeps this area clean. Foul of the foot has a distinctive and unpleasant smell.

38. Butts: semi-permanent low structures in a line across known flight paths of driven birds.

39. Old crop: grain from the previous year's harvest. The highest price in most years would be 'old crop' delivered in July.

40. Binder: a machine that cut the crop earlier and tied it in sheaves; it was then put up in stooks and allowed to mature.

41. Stooked: the sheaves of cereal are stacked heads up against each other in groups of six or eight. The resultant stack is the stook. The verb is stooking the sheaves.

42. Thrashing box: more or less a stationary combine harvester. They are generally powered by a steam traction engine. They travel the agricultural show circuit now, to show our urban cousins how it used to be.

43. Topped: mown down to no more than two inches high; keep it like a lawn then they will eat it – becoming cheaper to feed.

44. Glass: barometer.

45. Butt rot: rotting from the bottom up. It afflicts most types of trees, not just hardwoods; Southern Beech, Western Hemlock suffer badly in Devon – they seem free of it in Hampshire.

46. Compound: fertiliser containing the three main plant foods – nitrogen, phosphate and potash with this particular sowing in a ratio of 20N 10P 10K. Straight fertiliser would be the same constituents but in single make-up; ICI Nitram for example is straight nitrogen.

47. French drain: A large ditch cut into the soil, up to four feet deep and perhaps three feet wide; in the bottom is laid a six-inch land drain, covering this a layer of heather cut from the

New Forest, on top of this the ditch is part filled with flints, picked up from the chalky ground, then covered in soil.

48. Guns: people who do the shooting are known as guns.

49. Flushed : the act of scaring the game into the air. The quarry was never shot on the ground – there has to be 'law' given.

50. Partridge Manor: a shoot where partridges were the only game preserved, with this preservation came brown hares so the manor was one of the major coursing grounds.

51. Duck flighting: shooting duck in a tidal situation, natural and difficult.

52. Beaters' cart: generally a tractor and trailer with a covered top; due to the distances involved the keepers and beaters are driven to where they are to start the beat.

53. Ride-nets: very fine nets strung across rides in woodland – lethal to sparrow hawks but a little indiscriminate.

54. Ugly logs: logs which are large and unsplittable are always known as ugly – they are usually reduced in size by a chainsaw.

55. Polled: de-horned physically or had their horns bred out of them.

56. Haulm: the part of the potato plant which shows above ground, green and sappy. It is removed before lifting in case there are any blight spores on it – which might in turn fall onto the potatoes.

57. Rose end up: potatoes have an upside and a downside, look at each end of any potato and you will see small indenta-

tions in one end. This is where the haulm grows from – the rose end.

58. Dogged off: pushing game back home with dogs – usually pushing your game from a neighbour's land with his permission.

59. Rood: quarter of an acre – 1210 square yards.

TINKERS, TOWNIES AND TOFFS

A Countryman's Thoughts

Rod Brammer

Enq: www.kboauthors.com

BEFORE WE START...

Until education was dumbed down so grievously, most young people would have known who Jethro Tull and Charles Townsend were. People were closer to their rural roots then, and agriculture was also more valued. It was the country's basic industry. In short... it fed them. And if I say that Tull invented the seed drill and Townsend the four-course rotation of crops, by the introduction of the turnip into the equation, would that jog some memories? No? Then let me explain.

Tull's seed drill allowed for the accurate placement of seed corn in rows, thereby allowing for hoeing to take place, which in turn, because of the decreased competition from weeds, increased yields. Townsend's four-course rotation, or even Norfolk four-course rotation, allowed for the widening of the rotation of crops by the planting of turnips, generally in place of a year's 'fallow'. Fallow is just growing nothing on a piece of land, taking the opportunity to rest it, doing nothing more to it than some weed control.

Soon, there were thousands of acres being drilled with turnips, being grazed by millions of sheep, producing wool and meat, but also, just as importantly, providing manure, which increased the wheat, barley and oat tonnages. Sheep's wool became the driving force of the new manufacturing economy, as coal made the Industrial Revolution possible; wool made possible this country's expansionist foreign policy, and all this from a seed drill. And an idea in the early eighteenth century.

CHAPTER ONE
(January)

Given there are another three hundred and sixty-four days to choose from, one is forced to wonder why anyone would choose the first of January as the start of the year. Then, to compound the folly, call it a 'New Year', because, in truth, there is very little 'new' about it. January 1 is in the depth of winter and the worst of that season is generally yet to come. The 'New Year' should surely be when the first signs of spring are there for us to see. Let us go through a year together, watching the birds, listening to the trees, noting the miracles in every pond and stream, then you can choose for yourself that which is your new year.

My completely unscientific, unrepresentative survey suggested that most people's idea of spring is daffodils. Not one person suggested snowdrops, pussy willow or even rooks. Spring is always a long time occurring. The signs are there, back in February, uplifting for those who see and note them, but for those who miss these signs, there is only waiting.

It used to be that practically every parish in England could boast a rookery, to a greater or lesser extent. The demise of the English elm, through disease, brought an end to this. How many pictures have been painted of rooks in elm trees? Now they are gone along, initially, with lots of the rooks. Their numbers are growing again and only last February, I saw what, for me, is the first awakening of spring; a rook, flying with a twig in its beak, carrying it back to its rookery, to effect repairs on last year's nest. My observation is that rooks now mainly nest in mature ash trees. I wonder what made them choose the ash? Probably because the trees grow in groups and rooks need the company of other rooks. They are super intelligent birds with a social hierarchy of their own.

If you study a rookery for long enough, you will soon begin to see what I mean. The birds that are in charge seem to have the right to steal from the others, taking choice twigs to mend or improve their own nests. They intervene in the squabbles of others, attempting to keep the peace. It is very difficult to recognise one rook from another, so a bird becomes 'the rook from the second nest on the left'. Rather than the actual rook, it becomes the nest whence it came.

Spoken about and written about, more often than actually seen, is something dubbed 'the Rooks' Parliament'. I have seen it once in all my years of watching nature. I confess I did not know exactly what was happening but happen it did. The rooks in question came from a large rookery in the tiny hamlet of Calmore in Hampshire. The elms which housed the nests were in a field next to HMS *Safeguard* at Tatchbury Mount.

As I remember it, it was middle to late summer. Certainly, it was past haymaking time and the rooks had been noisy for the previous two days, hanging around the rookery instead of going out to forage in the local fields. Their calls in obvious agitation were enough to cause remarks to be made in the local pub. Most put it down to a coming change in the weather. Those who really knew the rook didn't hold with this. The birds had not spent anytime 'basket weaving' above the rookery trees after all. The excitement was higher pitched, more intense. The Parliament, when it happened, was over in minutes, the rooks dividing into two roughly similar groups. Half stayed, calling from the elms, the others pitched onto the fields.

How it happened I did not see, but suddenly there were four birds together in a large space, surrounded by the others on the ground. There was some calling from those on the ground until, as one, they lifted themselves up into the elms. The four birds in the centre remained for a few moments, before flying north.

What it was about I could not say with any certainty and there did not seem to be any animosity involved. I like to think the four birds were selected by the others, to fly off and start a new rookery. Perhaps they were told to build their nests in the ash trees. Most country people know that rooks can see the future in some measure.

CHAPTER TWO
(February)

There can surely be no difficulty about getting up with the dawn in February. It doesn't really get properly light until after seven and on an overcast day it can be dark until eight. With the dawn comes bird song, not much I grant you, but reliably robins, wrens and the mistle thrush. The mistle thrush, like the rook, is an early nest builder. The hen bird does the building, whilst the cock sits in the top-most branches, practising his fluty song, warning others that this is his patch. Even in the roughest weather, the mistle thrush will perch in swinging branches, in the teeth of a gale, and sing. Early on the song is short, four or five different notes, repeated to the point of tedium. By the end of the month, the song is lengthened – spring is coming. His song is longer, more varied and beautiful. Beautiful, because it is loud and clear, an octave lower that the song of its cousin, the song thrush, but as you listen your confidence grows. The year is waking. So, an early nester and an early riser, the song of the mistle thrush, delivered virtuoso, wakes the rooks, who in turn wake the sleeping fields, woods and hedgerows.

Though often described as the 'cruellest month', in some years February throws up ten days to a fortnight of dry warm sunny weather, which always bamboozles the frogs and the newspaper editors.

Frogs make their way in droves to the nearest ponds, wanting to mate. They do, and buckets of spawn are produced, literally millions of eggs, but alas, the sunny days of February mean freezing clear nights. The spawn is frozen and dies.

The newspaper editors, perhaps in desperation for a story, send their journalists into the rural areas to see this phenomenon of global warming: to get eyewitness statements about the destruction of our ecosystems. For a few pints of best bitter, most countrymen will give them what they want. 'Never know'd the like, straight I ain't.' They will agree with the journalist's London editor: 'It's this 'yere global warm-up, Sir, you buy me another pint, an' I'll show you primroses and bluebells that 'ave flowered already.'

Journalists fall for all this every time and are duly led to some dingley dell, where there are flowers in profusion. The fact that the tiny dell is on a south-facing slope, out of the wind and catching all the sun, means nothing to them. In some cases, the primroses have been flowering since the previous October. Next day, photographs appear in the newspapers of flowers in bloom, ostensibly six weeks earlier than normal, with stories of impending doom. The capital flooding... Norfolk under a foot of sea water from melting glaciers... but the landlord of *The Three Tuns* smiles quietly with a couple of his regulars: 'Whose turn is it next?' he laughs.

It is small wonder that our forebears worshipped the sun, even in February when it sends down but little warmth. It does give us a spiritual lift. Our animals feel the same, I know. The dairy cows, yarded since October, hang over the metal gates to catch the rays, until they are let out 'for a gentle wander', to pick about on what grass there is. They are always pleased, teetering across the frozen ground, like fat old ladies crossing a shingle beach towards the tide line. If cows could laugh, they would then. They have a good sense of humour, full of mischief. They soon enough give up foraging, preferring to lie down in the sun warming their fat, red roan backs, cudding, belching and breaking wind, filling the air with the milky smell of their breath.

February, cruel maybe, capricious certainly towards the end of the month and seemingly unwilling to acknowledge that winter is leaving the stage. Sometimes the weather does an about-face. Cold rain, sleet and snow can sweep down from the northeast, peppering the furrows of the spring cereal ground with ice, which hangs on the north-facing ridges, cold and barren.

'Hanging about for more, I shouldn't wonder,' a pundit may observe, made melancholy by too much darkness.
''T won't last,' another observes sagely. 'I seen a brood of ducks yesterday.'

With the passage of a week, they can both be proved right. A sharp frost after cold rain can kill young ducks. Two days later, another brood of ducklings appear, sunning themselves and sheltering behind their mother in the weak, watery sun. Meanwhile, a fat pregnant brown rat feeds on the body of a duckling recently frozen and an eel feeds on the one that tumbled into the feeder stream when the gripping cold halted its tiny heart beat.

As February turns to March, the garden cock blackbirds take on a darker hue. Or is it that their beaks change to a brighter orange, contrasting with the black feathers more sharply? They spend their time chasing others from the lawns, hopping in long low leaps, aggressive now that sun has stirred their hormones. The winners, those with the longest leaps it seems, establish their territories and drive away anything that comes near. Even yard cats are not immune from attack. They skulk from the yard with a look on their flat faces which proclaims the world has gone mad – just because of a little sun.

Meanwhile their much dowdier cousins, the song thrushes, have got on and built their mud-cupped nest in the ivy on the side of the house. Two blue jewels, with black spots, have already been laid. They shine like tiny eggs from the Russian master jeweller, easy pickings for the black-hearted magpies. The countryman sets his Larsen trap. The decoy-bird, over-wintered in the luxury of the barn, now must do his Judas duty, calling his black and white race to destruction.

Failing in this duty, his life becomes forfeit, and another bird is procured, preferably from another part of the country. A stranger works best. Is it because he chatters in a different accent? A countryman from Lancashire speaks differently from a Devon man, so why not the same with birds? Listen to the other birds. A Devon blackbird has a somewhat different song from a blackbird that greets the dawn in Hampshire. Obviously, both are recognised as being blackbirds, but they are both subtly at variance.

A week seems very much longer at February's end. We are impatient now for the promised longer evenings, when tea can be taken in the daylight. The song thrush now has five eggs. She sits tightly, fed by her mate and only her beak and tail appear above the edge of their nest. But do not stare, rather pretend you are not even looking in her direction. She will be more comfortable. Almost paralysed by 'broody fever', the song thrush is vulnerable now. The countryman values her work in the garden with the snails and slugs, and glories in her mate's song in the mornings. So he keeps a special eye on her, watching for predators who have been watching themselves for an opportunity to take her eggs. The regular movements by the parent birds into the ivy, where the nest is barely hidden, will have been noted. The grey squirrel may wait until the blue eggs hatch; the tiny featherless babies are a toothsome morsel. The sparrow hawk will have seen the comings and goings, waiting its chance to snatch one of the thrushes from the air, before stripping the still alive bird's speckled breast of its delicate meat. Surely the cruellest thing in nature; and one which no countryman will countenance without some sanction.

***

The Game Shooting comes to an end now. The second of February generally arrives with the open spaces carpeted with cock pheasants parading themselves, mocking their erstwhile hunters. There is always great amusement when a cock bird, conspicuous by some special feathering, reappears. Having skulked about hidden all through the shooting season, he now feels free to disport himself in front of the hen pheasants.

We had a dark green Melanistic cock bird locally, a strikingly beautiful bird, the bottle green of his wings and rump iridescent in the light. A remarkably strong flyer who knew how many beans made five, he overflew the guns for a couple of seasons at a wholly prodigious height, and remained safe. Thereafter, on shoot days, he would ensconce himself in the chicken run, socialising with the Light Sussex hens, avoiding the beaters. For half a dozen springs, 'The Green Man' would show himself during the first week of February, gather up six or seven hens, take them to the windbreak in Lydgate's Field and raise his family.

One year he was challenged by a common-looking ring-necked pheasant. 'The Green Man' fought and slew him, leaving himself exhausted and injured. The very next day, another young blood arrived, killed 'The Green Man', took his hens to add to his own plurality, but he was never the same. So ordinary, we did not notice or mourn his passing when it came.

CHAPTER THREE
(March)

'March comes in like a lion': well, it does sometimes. However it comes, six weeks on, it will be spring. The light now is different. The sun has just a touch of warmth early in the month, but joy of joys must be the picture when the light shows forcefully upon a dark cloud crossing the downs, with the larch trees in between, showing the merest dusting of the palest green, as the new needles begin to burst from their buds. Is it a trick of this new light, or is that really some green upon the stark, bare hawthorn hedgerow? That stretch in the corner out of the wind is always the first to show leaf, despite the raw damp cold, even when the new grass growth looks blue-grey in the east wind. The hawthorn, sucking juice and sustenance from the cold earth, says: 'Spring is with us.'

The river, the goddess in our lives, begins to fine down, clearing as the water from the winter-bourns higher up the valley, push the last of the debris and detritus of the winter before it. The yellow gravel of the riverbed begins to show in deeper water now; the silt and washings that lingered through December in the estuary now rest in great ridged bars near Calshot, until the dredger comes to clear them.

Below Romsey, the countryman watches the bank-high water as it flows down to the Solent; at the new grass on the top of the banks; in the deeper pools looking dark and acidic. He sees the few dead salmon still coming down from the spawning beds, huge great fish, the like of which are seldom caught. They tumble over in the current, rotting, covered in fungus, stinking if they touch the air. Not all of them die after they spawn. Sometimes the countryman sees a live fish, fungus covering its flanks, drifting down the current, just below the surface.

Facing upstream, resting sometimes in the shallows, its thin form half out of the water. Maybe, by tea-time this day, it will reach the salt water and the cleansing salt will seep between the huge scales, lifting the white, clinging strings of fungus, cleaning and renewing. Given luck, and a strong ebb, the fish may pass the silt banks at Calshot, reach the Solent proper and begin to feed again. Such fish as these spend time on the Greenland Shelf, feeding, patrolling, until the unstoppable urge comes again, to return to their river of birth, massive fish now, driven by the nature of their being to spawn again to renew numbers, propagating their race.

The river now runs with bank-high clarity. Only in the very deepest parts is the bottom not visible through the bright clear stream. It is fascinating to peer down into the depths, almost like an interloper. Stay hidden and still, watch as the fish go about their lives. You may be lucky to see a shaft of spring sunshine probe the depths. A yellow flickering spotlight which most of the fish avoid, but not that most beautiful of fish, the grayling. They are nearing their own spawning. The cock fish, with their iridescent greenish flanks, splashes of red on their sail-like dorsal fins, play in the shafts of light: beautiful fish, with their own *joie de vivre*.

As the light picks up, the small birds do not come to the bird table in such numbers. No longer can we enjoy the profusion of their colours. Two weeks ago they looked like a casket of spilled jewels, feasting on the food put out for them, but now they are busy with their own domestic chores: house building, breeding, feeding more intermittently. The countryman listens, noting where they have their nests, knowing that the vermin in the area are doing the same thing. The wrens that have built their complex nest high in the vaulted, cathedral-like roof of the grain dryer have chosen well.

Their ball-shaped home with its side entrance sits on the cross member of the elevator shaft, sixty feet above the floor. The yard cats, whose job it is to keep the mice and rats in check, know the nest is there but cannot reach it. The tiny wrens sing their song, a song so loud from such a tiny bird, it echoes through the buildings, disturbing the roosting barn owls, who live in a purpose-built nesting box, in the highest curving gable of the barn. They peer out with their flat, clown-like faces, guarding their first egg of the season.

No magpie would risk his life trying to take it. The wrens shelter behind their watchful presence, for the owls will not tolerate anything bigger than a sparrow in their barn. Nature – perfect in its synergy.

Perceptibly now spring creeps up on us, and the weather the mainspring of conversation. What does it hold for us?
'I just wish it would rain, sometimes.' This is what a young lady, who had moved to Australia, said to me. There was a tear on her cheek at that moment and I wished I had not asked what her weather had been like.

We, in these islands, talk about 'the weather'. I suppose because it is rarely settled, rarely extreme and rarely these days forecast correctly by the Met Office. This is of no matter to the countryman. He doesn't need to listen to the television, with the young lady reading out what is going to be our lot. He knows better than she because he has a mass of accumulated knowledge gained over the years. He looks at the cloud patterns, maybe just a glance. He may not know the names of various clouds, but he knows their effect. It is rarely a question of standing to look. Rather, the countryman goes about his normal work of the day, noting, even subconsciously, what is happening around him. The redwings, flying back to Scandinavia, send down their *chacking* calls. These same calls foretold of cold weather last November when birds arrived here. What they tell him now is that there will be no bad weather coming down from the north in the next few days.

The countryman is at one with his surroundings. As he left the house that morning, the slight westerly breeze, laden with moisture and salt, dampened his shirt collar. It would surely rain before lunchtime.

Winter rain falls steadily for hours, cold and depressing. It moves slowly, the fronts seeming to dwell exactly where they are not needed. Rarely is it dramatic or beautiful. Watch with me, if you will, a weather front rushing from the south-west. There is no hurry. It's a dozen or so miles away. Watch as it bubbles and froths: pale grey-blue clouds making sculptures in the sky. That which was a gentle breeze, now stiffens its sinews, throwing shut a stable door with a crash. The smaller birds scatter to their favourite sheds and the yard cat moves moodily to shelter in the log store.

At our backs, the sun shines towards the approaching front. The underside of the cloud glows in a golden line, a reflection from the sea beneath it. Clearer now, curtains of rain dwell beneath the cloud. The rooks, busy picking over recently spread dung on the stubbles, lift as one, heading for the lee of the wood. A mile away, the conifer windbreak suddenly, violently, bends before the sobbing wind: closer, a wisp of hay from that put out for the cattle, picks up, spinning in the air, then catches in the lower branches of an oak tree.

The first splashes of rain rattle like spent shot across the yard buildings to be overtaken by a sweet-smelling deluge, falling in sheets, overflowing the gutters, whipping the yard puddles to foam, drumming on barn roofs. The storm passes over the down-lands, falling in driven curtains, bending before the wind, like sails of a spectral sailing ship driving hard.

On the terracotta pantiles of the old workshop a wood pigeon lays haphazardly on its breast, its wings spread, the flight feathers pushed far apart like a lady's fan. The rain gently cleaves the dirt and muck from the nursery nest that has stained and accumulated on it. The wood pigeon's beauty is so often missed: the pink-flushed breast, topped by the snow-white collar, the iridescent blues and greens of its shoulders. If it was shown on television wildlife programmes, while still noted as a significant pest to the countryside, it is at least a significantly beautiful pest.

To those who live in the towns and only see the wood pigeon in the public parks, dirt-covered, fat couch potatoes, let me say its country cousin is the Aston Martin of birds, masters of the air like few others. As a sporting bird it has no equal; grey partridge may push it close, but 'paddies' have predictability about them.

Roost shooting autumn pigeons, to me, is the absolute cream of shooting sports. Do them justice though, please don't shoot them with light shot; fours or fives are best. When you hold the aerial athlete in your hand, please know you are holding something wonderful... and tell the cook not to overdo them.

***

Spring has arrived. The softness of the air tells us so. The song thrush youngsters have fledged. The mother has hidden them in various bushes around the garden and now both parents are running themselves ragged feeding them. The would-be predators have been dealt with. The major ones, the very worst offenders, the yard cats, have been caught up and imprisoned in the old tennis court. Their incarceration will last until mid-August. The chain-link fencing, sunk into thick tarmac, cannot be breached. The overhead space is closed by a small mesh net.

It was made thus through the Second World War. There being then no fripperies such as tennis, the pure-bred hens lived there. Now it is the feline prison, to stop them killing the young fledglings. There are various shelters for them, a fairly hefty ash log to sit on and sharpen their claws. They are not ever happy about their situation, but tell me, please, when are cats ever happy?

Now, when the sun shines, the earth smokes gently with the steam of evaporation, the roadside banks become greener, suddenly spring sowing is with us. The ploughing that was done last autumn, and left to weather, is crumbly and drying. The soil temperature has risen. It used to be said, that if you could sit 'bare bottomed' on the soil without discomfort, then it was warm enough to sow. These days, a stricter science is used in the form of a soil thermometer, more accurate certainly, but less colourful.

However the soil temperature is checked, before drilling can commence the autumn-ploughed ground will be walked over, studied and kicked to see how it crumbles. Is the top ground, white with the chalk beneath it, studded with flints that 'grow' over winter, washed clean by the rains, going to need a harrowing? The furrows left by the ploughs have collapsed, not furrows now, just regular small ridges. The wind, rain and frosts have done their work. The action of the seed drill's coulters will do the rest. If the weather holds, in ten days, the job will be done. If it doesn't, then who knows?

In the farm's yards all is quiet throughout the day. For the first time in weeks all that can be heard is the noise of the sparrows squabbling or cleaning themselves in the sandy dust, lying in the ridges of the concrete. The clanging, ringing note of a spanner being dropped in the workshop is the only confirmation that someone is about.

As the days pass, the sounds of the tractor exhausts can be heard in the yards, coming from the high downs where the land is lighter and more friable. Then, onto the lower heavier soil where machinery has to work harder and the exhaust notes are more laboured. The pace never seems to slow, the drilling going on far into the evenings and darkness, until only the pea ground is left to do, later in the middle of next month.

The tiny ridges on the otherwise flat surfaces of the drilled land make it look like a dark-grey corduroy cloth. The ring rollers do this, pushing down on the soil, pressing it around the barley seed, snug in its warm bed, keeping the moisture in. Already on the high downs, the seed is shooting, sending up slender green spikes in serried ranks that blend into a green mist further away.

The brown hares, disturbed by the field work, gradually reclaim the high ground. They look huge now with no cover in which to hide themselves. The rolled ground, so flat it accentuates their size, will soon become their playground as they start their mating rituals.

It is around this time that baby rabbits begin to show themselves; tiny, innocent, fluffy bunnies – who could deny their charm? Despite everything being thrown in their direction, *Myxie*, shooting, netting, snaring, dogs, normal predation, they still thrive. I do not know a real countryman who doesn't greet the sight of a fleeing rabbit with a somewhat wry smile. Wasn't it the humble rabbit that fed him when times were hard? The much talked about but seldom now actually seen rabbit pie. Rabbit and starling stew, with the addition of a ham knuckle – only those who have known a ration book will remember this culinary delight.

A tube of shot from a twelve-bore – five-shot pellets are best – fired into a flock of starlings going to roost, generally produces twenty to thirty birds. Gather them up. They are the cottager's manna from heaven. Skin the breasts, remove the dark red medallions of flesh from each side of the keel bone and wonder why such fare is no longer eaten. The robust health of the cottager's children is testament to nutritional value.

In past times, the successful completion of the spring sowing would be marked by a celebration around the time of the Spring Equinox. This, to me, is the New Year. The downs are covered with the green shoots of the cereal crops. The larch trees are in bud. The brown hares are acting out their stylised rituals by having pretend boxing matches.

They are too gentle a creature to properly fight. They run in tight circles, chasing each other, stop suddenly, turn and start to 'box'. If you watch closely, they seldom actually touch each other. It is generally assumed these boxing matches are the males sparring. I would say it was the females. Let me qualify this. In the early fifties there were two easily identifiable hares on the farm. One had had her left ear split, probably on barbed wire. The other was missing a front paw. Neither injury seemed to bother either one of them. They mixed easily with the other hares and generally went about their business in the normal fashion. As a child I used to watch them through my grandfather's field glasses. Both of these hares had leverets, which they fed at night, moving between them in turn.

There being no buzzards in Hampshire in those days to kill leverets, all the hares on the farm were very strictly preserved, for no other reason than their mystical beauty. At any one time, there would have been around three hundred, scattered between the arable land, the grassland and woods at a more than sustainable level of one hare per fifteen to sixteen acres. Sadly they are no longer with us, driven out and killed by the intransigence and ignorance of what country people refer to as the Bird Police.

Buzzards, immigrants from the West Country, spread across the county, killing ever more leverets. Hares are now a rarity at home. What was not, was winged vermin. To counter this there were annual vermin shoots. There was great co-operation on these shoots. Gamekeepers, foresters and their friends would turn up from all over the county, and in return, our keepers and those from the next door estate would return the favour.

The day would start with forty to fifty people, others joined as their work commitments at home allowed. They would encircle a large area, and on the sound of a whistle or horn, the circle would move inward. Generally there would be at least three sets of drey-poking poles, long lengths of aluminium, which were used to push out squirrel dreys and their occupants to the waiting group of guns closest to the woods.

Jays, crows, magpies, sparrowhawks, all would suffer the same fate. In fact, anything that preyed on the songbirds, waders and partridges. A cry of 'Tobey!'[*1] would put the people nearest to the cry on their mettle, waiting to see the russet-red skulking form of a fox caught above ground. If it stayed above ground it paid immediately for its temerity. If it went to ground, the earth would be marked, to be dealt with later that same day.

As the circle tightened, the headman would blow his whistle twice, which meant 'in the air shots', or outside the circle only. For decades this system of wholesale vermin control was employed. It produced a wholly balanced outcome. The songbirds were in profusion. What a pity that protest and ignorance put an end to it. These protests are born of ignorance, an ignorance that I have but little patience with. Urban people will never accept that there is a degree of killing which has to take place, to keep a balance. It is now euphemistically referred to as 'culling' or 'management' to save the town people's sensitivities.

The fact remains that predators must be killed to save the predated species at a level which allows them to survive and breed.

***

As the month grows older the first of the fox cubs are born. Who could imagine such charming playful balls of fluff could change into the destructive pests they are destined to become? The female is now referred to as a 'wet vixen', in normal speak, she is suckling cubs and is now inviolable. A countryman would not kill her. The consequences of doing so would be the starvation of the cubs below ground. This is not as the anti-s think and say, a way of preserving foxes to hunt later, but common humanity.

Foxes are extraordinarily clever. I would put them in the same bracket as a Border collie. They understand cause and effect, and can therefore plan ahead. Rural foxes know that man is their enemy. They also know that they have to live in the same space as man. This makes them very careful. When the cubs are born, initially the vixen stays underground with them. The dog fox, at the start, can keep her fed enough to produce milk for the cubs and maintain her body weight.

As they grow, this becomes more difficult for the dog as the mother and cubs need ever more food. He will now begin to hunt earlier in the evenings, later after dawn. The dairyman may see him in the early light, either hunting the hedgerow, sometimes trotting across open ground with a rabbit or a hen pheasant in his mouth.

The fox knows he has nothing to fear from this human in a white overall, calling his cows to him. The fox is sometimes startled when the human speaks to him: 'Morning Tobey, had a good night, how's the wife and kids?' Most working countrymen hold the fox in high regard, especially farm workers. Why shouldn't they? Foxes are the bane of the gamekeeper's life. After all, it was only one generation ago that a farm worker caught catching a rabbit to feed his family would be 'up before the bench' and fined heavily. Two generations ago, for the same offence, a farm worker could lose his home, job, perhaps be fined as well as spending seven days in the local lock-up. Further back the evils of 'transportation' came into play – for a rabbit!

So it is of not much consequence if the snivelling wretch that is the gamekeeper is being robbed blind by Tobey. The fox might well be reported to the hunt for future reference, but not to the gamekeeper.

Today's gamekeepers are a different breed. They no longer seem to be naturalists, any more than today's poachers. Keepers today are little more than poultry keepers, rearing thousands of birds to put over paying guns. Commercial shooting arrived a score of years ago. It brings vast sums of money for the ailing rural economy and to my mind that is the only good that comes of it.

The life of a gamekeeper has changed enormously; no longer a servant of a landowner because the landowner has most likely let his shooting rights to some city chap with lots of money. The gamekeeper now works for money, his job specification nothing more than the bare bones of what gamekeeping used to be. It could be said, twenty years ago, that a properly keepered estate had a diversity of wildlife and a large songbird population, principally because the keepers kept the vermin in check.

These days the main, and sometimes only, vermin control carried out is driving around at night shooting foxes with the aid of powerful spotlights and rifles. Trapping seems to be a thing of the past. For example, I went to the local field sports shop just recently for some Fen traps. They had to order in my request. The shop no longer carried them as a matter of course: 'Not so much call for them these days,' I was told, which about says it all.

An irony of this huge increase in the rearing of game birds is that there are far too many of them now. They are worth very little, certainly not enough to make it worthwhile poaching them. Of course the old-fashioned, romantic idea of a man poaching a pheasant for his family to eat, has gone. Poaching was done by gangs of desperate men, ready to risk gaol and a fight with gamekeepers. Not now though. Who would risk heavy fines and prison for so little reward? A pheasant in feather is worth not even one pound.

Now it seems that those who made a living by raiding the covers at night, these days make their money by raiding farms, stealing quad bikes, Land Rovers, tractors and even fuel. Just recently a trailer-load of silage bales was stolen from a farm locally; they are only of use to another farmer. I leave you to ponder the morality of this particular crime.

For me there are places which give me quietude. I hope you have such places, somewhere that relaxes your mind. Even as a child, they were special places and years later, when abroad for example, I would find myself yearning for them, thinking about them, trying to conjure up the smell of them.

One such place, probably the most relaxing of all, is the water meadow along the bottom of a river valley, always green, full of wildlife and the sound of water. Long ago, when the river ran free of man's interference, before anybody knew how to control its waywardness, the valley bottom would have been a soggy place indeed. For centuries the river would have flooded, dropping its sediment and alluvial mud far out from its normal course. This, and the river cutting down into the earth, would have given it its natural course, taking the line of least resistance, meandering its way toward the sea.

As the valley reached the estuary, it was perhaps wrong to refer to it as a valley. Here, the movement of the river was governed by something more powerful than itself – the tides. Twice a day the river was checked in its southerly flight to the sea. It had to go somewhere so it spread sideways, out to the sides of the valley, dropping its mud and silt – forming mud flats when the tide retreated, forming at its head an area of land which gradually got higher, high enough to dry out in the summer. This area, where hundreds of acres were taken up and farmed, then improved with land drains, eventually formalised into water meadows with a system of carriers and feeders, sluiced so the flowing water could be directed, stopped, rushed through and able, finally, to overflow into the meadows.

There were two reasons for passing running water over meadows. One or two inches of fast-running water stopped the land getting frozen solid: it kept it warmer in fact. Secondly, the nutrients the water carried were deposited on the sward, making for early grass. It was a very clever system, employing a lot of labour, and that was the problem, as labour got more expensive. The 'drowners', as they were known, faded away. The water meadows fell into disrepair, sluices collapsed, feeders silted up and became choked with water-weed and flags, and perhaps overgrown with shrubby trees, ideal for wildlife.

These days the irrigation channels, the carriers, and feeders, are just cleaned with a mechanical digger at the beginning of winter. The resultant spoil is spread on spring barley ground to rot down. Maybe two or three loads will be dumped on the kitchen garden and the tiny particles of chalk washed down from the north of the county sweeten the soil everywhere it touches. The streams soon settle back down; by now in March, they run freely, the water so clean and so clear, it is fit to drink. Try some and taste for yourself.

This is what our forebears drank, so clear it looks blue in the cup, so cold it makes your teeth and throat ache. Your drink will taste of the chalk that is dissolved in the water. It is the same chalk that gives the natives their great dense bones, wide shovel-like hands which can cleft fencing stakes from oak trunks for a whole day, or gentle a spring lamb from its mother's womb. The native, pure-bred females, still exhibit the genes of their Jute ancestry, long-boned with good teeth, red gold hair and straight noses, splashed with freckles. Their ancestors saw the clarity of the water and the denseness of the sward beneath their feet, and decided to stay.

The water meadows are a place of calmness, a place of fat cattle and sleek horses. My mind was as near stilled as ever in my life, when I walked this beautiful place. Come then, enjoy with me the delicate ambience of these ancient meadows in early spring.

With the water so clear, with no real depth to it, we keep the spring sunshine to our front, lest our shadows, which we have not seen for months, fall across the water and frighten the fish. They are wary, for the weed has not properly grown to give them a place to hide. If you look under the opposite bank, especially near any old tree roots, you may see a chub, that 'most fearful of fishes', as Walton called them.

They look huge in the feeder stream, their great silver-bronze flanks, solid muscle, ready to power them away to safety. In the main river such fish as these, upwards of five pounds, would be a troublesome nuisance, eating the salmon parr and young trout. Here, they were a handy indication of the otter population, far too big for an otter to eat at one sitting. If they did catch one, the remains, perfectly skinned, would be found on the bank.

Otters were never as scarce as the pseudo-conservationists would have the general population believe; proper country people knew this, so did not worry. The problem with otters is that they require real skill to actually observe them and see the signs of where they are and such skills are not usually found amongst the pseuds. I stated this once in a letter to a field sports magazine and it was immediately challenged by a professor of natural history. I didn't know there were such things. However, the challenge was taken up. The said professor was shown she was in error, though she was, however, fun to be with.

About half a mile downstream from where the bridge crosses

the Blackwater at Ridge, there is the oldest part of the water meadow system. The river runs over a long concrete sill that was at some stage a set of substantial sluice gates. The river skips across the sill, to tumble into the pool below. Over the years this pool had acquired a depth of about seven feet. A large meadow carrier, coming down from Romsey, also empties into it. The carrier is only slightly smaller than the little Blackwater River and together the two waters mingle to join the main river just above Testwood.

This carrier has various names, none I think official. We always called it the Moggy Stream, because of the dozens of moorhens who chose the stream as their nesting place. It wasn't only moorhen, there were dabchicks, a few coots and along its edges curlew, snipe, woodcock and peewits. With the water meadow system trees were very few, a scrubby hawthorn here and there along some stream banks, more substantial alders, whose roots helped to support the banks and a few hazels. It was the only cover for hundreds of yards, so birds like snipe and peewits gravitated to them.

As we walk slowly upstream, the small green plank bridge, just up from the pool, was put there for the keeper to cross. Look out beyond the stream and there are tiny tracks, like roads leading to Piccadilly Circus across the short grass, all converging on the small bridge. The keepers aren't the only ones who use the bridge. These just barely worn tracks, or 'runs', as we call them, are from the foxes, hares and maybe otters that use the bridge. Look closely at the matt green-painted planks. A drag mark on the bridge has been made by the otter's tail, from sandy mud it picked up coming under the gate where the cattle go through to their hay racks.
Rather than keep walking, stop and watch from one of the scrubby hawthorns, blend yourself into its shape and look upstream. A fish makes a splashy rise. The sun, now warming the air, has made some fly life hatch, a cloud of gnats' dance in the

air above our hawthorn bush.

Upstream there is another splash, closer than the last. Wait for the next one, obvious now as the splashes and dimples on the surface drift close. Hawthorn flies, a large cloud of the big bushy-looking insects, their legs dangling, seeming unconnected to their bodies, are drifting on the breeze toward us, several hundred of them. A barely noticeable breeze brings them closer till they are with us, flying around our faces, dropping in the stream in dozens. The trout slash and rush them in something approaching a feeding frenzy. The frenzy turns to panic with the trout throwing themselves out of the water, as a bow wave, like an ocean liner, carves through the melee.

Briefly, a tan-coloured fish tail, eight inches across, shows above the surface. The ripples flatten out, a moorhen upstream explodes from the stream's surface as a pike passes, returning to its lie. There is virtual silence as the world collects itself, only the shortened sound of our breathing as we stare transfixed at the small streak of blood, red in the clear water, and then a curlew calls and brings our minds forward into the present.

Pike spawn at this time of the year and very often you will chance to see a large hen fish escorted by three or four small cock fish, called Jack Pike. The hen, when ready, will shed her eggs in the weeds, the escorts will drop their milt on them (they are fertilised by this). The mating process is over. At this point, the hen fish may well grab one of the cock fish and swallow it. Catching it crossways in her mouth, she waits till it is dead then turns it to swallow, head first.
As a sport fish, they are absurdly easy to catch; even large pike never seem to learn what to avoid. They are not welcome in a trout river. The modern idea is that they only take the weak fish. Forget that: they are exceptionally aggressive predators and will grab anything small enough to go down or fit in their amazing jaws. Tales of voracious pike are legion; some are true, most

are not, I'm afraid.

Ducklings, young moorhens, water voles, most certainly, pike will take and eat. Stories of full-grown mallard being taken are surely not true; killed maybe, grabbed then drowned, probably true. The pike would grab them from below, but by the time the pike discovered that the duck could not be swallowed, the duck would drown. Pike will take and swallow other fish, even their own kind seemingly a third of their size.

The only legend I can pass on as being true is that of Poppy's dog, a Yorkshire terrier named Lettie. Poppy – I shall not give her surname – was the result of a brother and sister, from an aristocratic family, discovering sex. Poppy was a tall pre- Raphaelite beauty who always dressed in the best of London fashion. Every spring and summer in diaphanous dresses, in winter beautifully cut tweed suits, always with the best of millinery fashion. She was oft times an incongruous sight, walking through the woods in strappy sandals and a chiffon dress, up to her ankles in spring mud and happy in her own world.

On the morning in question, we were returning from early morning cubbing, a bright blowy day at the back end of August. As we came down the lane towards the old stable block, we could see Poppy and the terrier chasing the first of the falling red and gold leaves of autumn. We did not see exactly what happened but the terrier probably saw a leaf land in the margins of the lake and went in after it. Poppy's maniacal screams were awful in that they sounded more like a donkey braying. Nature makes no concessions to madness.

The fish which had grabbed the dog washed up on the eel traps several days later, unable to eject the furry creature from its huge jaws because of its backward sloping teeth. It had probably died of exhaustion trying to rid itself from the dog. Separation was affected with a garden spade and for speed the tiny dog was buried in the mill meadow. The pike, stinking now, was kicked back into the river for it would at least feed the bass in the estuary.

As with most country boys, I had an airgun, an air rifle to be precise, a BSA Cadet Major. By today's standards it was relatively unsophisticated, open sights, beech-wood stock, not very pretty, but it was ferociously accurate. Firing a .177 waisted pellet, at about six hundred feet per second, it would deliver six and a half foot pounds of energy at twenty yards, so not very powerful, but it taught me so much. To be effective on a rabbit, I had to be within twenty yards of it and then hit it in the head. I spent hours crawling around hedgerows after vermin and in doing so saw so much of the wild life and how it reacted to me being there. How each species reacted to the other.

I quickly realised my ability to remain motionless was as important or even maybe more so than camouflage. When the smaller birds come flitting down the hedgerow in one direction, fleeing from something, remain very still. It may be the gamekeeper, but if the wood pigeon sitting on her eggs a few trees forward of you doesn't move, it probably isn't. But she does move, flapping noisily onto the outside of the hawthorn, pitching again. Move slowly – it maybe a magpie wanting to steal her eggs – and gently raise yourself. There on the tree top the black and white assassin sits, looking down into the tree, her head cocked on one side. The air rifle coughs, the magpie falls dead into the stream. That's perhaps another two dozen nests saved from its depredations. At this time of the year shooting and trapping magpies and other vermin are ongoing tasks for country boys. The men busy with field work tended to delegate the work to the boys, anything to save the song birds. A rich bounty is given for magpies, ten shillings per bird killed from some farms.

The air rifle taught me to move silently and very slowly; it gave me the chance to study and note everything around me. Nesting time for birds is the start of things growing. We were very lucky. We didn't have to wait for the daffodils in the garden to bloom, when wild daffodils were always earlier. Smaller than their flashy highly bred relations, they were exquisite jewels in the hedgerows of Hampshire. What became of them? They are not there now, sprayed out of existence with weed killer, no doubt. The only place I know where they still come every spring is in East Devon. Maybe farmers are more sympathetic to their surroundings in the West Country. I am unsure whether we have lost the wild daffodil. Are they bred plants that have naturalised?

The bulb catalogues sell daffodil bulbs suitable for naturalising. Quite close to a place called Ridge in Hampshire, there is an area of daffodils growing wild, naturalised if you want. They were planted there, on the edge of a wood in the 1930s, to mark where a young girl had died. They still come up every spring, beside the snowdrops which they were planted with. The daffodils are tiny blooms, the snowdrops a pure English variety, simple and lovely, as was the girl whose passing the flowers marked.

She died of consumption, walking from the family home not more than two gunshots away. Peggy sat down on a bank in the evening sun, among the primroses and died quietly. The joyous memory of her short simple life renewed every year in spring flowers.

CHAPTER FOUR
(April)

April, and the air is so clean and clear, it shines. This month must be the loveliest surely, but when May arrives, I think May is loveliest. April even smells different. The grass grows so quickly now it 'grows away' from the grazing cattle. Cows have to have the very best, before the grass goes stemmy. That way they produce the milk that smells sweet, full of cream and goodness. They stay out at night now, grazing the leafy ryegrass and clover swards for part of the night. Then they lie down and chew the cud.

The smell of regurgitated grass mingles with their milky breath, which in turn mingles with the mist risen from the river, so that it lingers in the air, sweet and clinging. At first light, as the herd is gathered up for milking, wagtails and starlings run about amongst the feet of the cattle, picking up insects and worms disturbed by the hooves of the dairy herd. To the layman the cattle are strung out in a long line, maybe three or four abreast, ambling gently towards their milking parlour, but as with most female groups, there is a strictly enforced hierarchy.

The Boss cows lead the herd in; the cows with the hardest heads which the others do not overtake, for fear of some very sore ribs. The dairyman will watch them closely: he knows each one individually, their funny traits, temperament, the way they walk. What he would be looking for is the first signs of the illness, hypomagnesaemia, a deficiency of magnesium in the blood. Even though there has been an additive in their feed-cake for weeks it can still strike.

It's an odd thing to see, a cow might perhaps stumble, which triggers the affliction. Suddenly the animal seems to lose control of its limbs, falling about as though drunk. Its colloquial name is Grass Staggers, which describes it accurately; as the affliction takes hold, the animal gets ever more agitated and aggressive. Other members of the herd may attack the sick animal, or flee in terror. Certainly, the dairyman needs to be aware that the milker may well attack him. Half a ton of fear-maddened Shorthorn is not something to trifle with. Eventually the animal will 'go down', either gently sinking to the ground, or collapsing dramatically on its side. A subcutaneous injection of magnesium puts the patient to rights in minutes.

A cow is very much a herd animal and will need to be kept well within sight and sound of her bovine friends. A kerf of hay to chew on is a good idea, until the disorientation leaves her. Dairy cows have a fairly hard life; a calf every year, then having to produce well over a thousand gallons of milk per lactation. This is extremely wearing on them. Provided they are looked after properly, they can go on for a dozen years, or the older pure breeds could. These days, if you see cows doing what they should do, grazing outside from spring to autumn, feel lucky. If they are any other colour than white and black, feel even more blessed.

Today's dairy herds are made up of Holstein cows who produce enormous amounts of milk, albeit with little to it. They are beautiful for their first and second calves. Thereafter they seem to 'fall out of bed'. They become bony, rangy, their udders become pendulous and by the age of six years most are in tins of dogmeat.

***

The swallows, who have been with us for two or three weeks, are joined this month by the house martins. Tiny black and white beauties, they flatter and honour us with their presence every year. At our Devon home they arrive around the time of the Queen's birthday; not too much gets done work-wise on that day, we all pretend to be busy, always with an eye to the sky. It is always a wonderful moment when the first martins arrive, sitting on the gutters staring down at the humans, chittering their funny song. As the day goes on, so the martins arrive in twos and threes. They rest on the roof for some minutes or chitter on the television aerial before going to feed above the ponds and marshy places.

Over the next week their numbers build gradually, until there are maybe one hundred of them swinging around the house and barns, hawking at insects above the muckheap. Soon they settle to nest-building and repair, the hose is run out onto the dusty yard, left at a trickle, so that muddy patches form. To the mud they gather, mixing it with their spittle, to make the tiny bricks they construct their exquisite nests with.

Where they build their nests show somehow that not only can these tiny scraps of bird navigate their way from Africa, but they also reason. Martins never, for example, build their nests on the west elevation, where the main of the bad weather comes from. They never build on the gun-room eaves or anywhere else where they are within reach of anyone over five feet.

As the month progresses, more adults arrive from Africa. These seem to take up residence in the man-made nests, put there for such a contingency. By June, the first fledglings are flying and it is wonderful to see perhaps three hundred martins flying around the house and yards. They are precious time wasters. They swoop around the barns, in and out of the doors, then dally on the wind or climb, then dive away, full of exuberance.

Such a large colony attracts the attention of predators. Sparrow hawks which by their daily attacks would decimate the martins; Great Spotted Woodpeckers will attack the nests, peck at them until they fall to the ground, leaving the fledglings as food for the woodpecker babies. My tolerance of such vermin is nought.

Spring, which just four weeks ago was a gentle prodding feeling spurring the world to wakefulness and energy, has become a beautiful taskmaster, pushy and urgent. It was time to sow the peas two weeks ago; rain and perhaps an over-enthusiastic cow dung application has made the fields in question a little claggy. Two years ago the fields had been down to a three-year grass ley, various ryegrasses plus red clover. This was ploughed in after a second cut of silage. The fields had been drilled with feed wheat, a feed variety call Hobbit as opposed to bread wheat, which would have been more normal, but the breeding sows would need to use these fields after the wheat so it needed to be harvested early. The bread wheat, by contrast, was cut later. The crop needed to take up another bag of nitrogen to fix the protein in the ears. This nitrogen was dropped into the crop by a tiny aircraft.

Around and about this time, in this particular year, the local Young Farmers Club lost their meeting place to the Townswomen's Guild. The town has grown quickly lately, no longer a sleepy market town, bypassed by the new roads; it had suddenly become The Place to Live. The consequence was the 'local' people were pushed out of the way by these thrusting, ill-mannered newcomers. The Young Farmers needed a meeting place, warm with electricity; they got it in the shape of a beautiful old granary, at the top end of the farm.

Quite near the town; eighty feet by twenty-five, resting on staddle stones, oak framed, elm clad, with lathe and lime plaster inside; thatched with reed from the estuary – it was and is a masterpiece of the rural architecture from Lord Nelson's time. Now it had a new lease of life; alterations were made to comply with safety laws, more windows, fire exits and the like.

What it did produce was a writ from the local council and about half a ton of old seed of various fodder crops. The writ was ignored; the seed was dropped into the field of nearly ripe Hobbit wheat by the tiny aircraft and forgotten about in the hurly-burly of late summer. There was one attempt by some of the local youth to break into the granary. The alarms and locks proved adequate, the would-be robbers picked up by the police, cautioned, then let go. Their names were published in the local press. The young men from the Young Farmers Club gave them something of a fairly strong physical warning when they caught up with them in the town's new coffee bar. Peace and quiet thereafter returned. The two cultures had difficulty living alongside each other for a few years though eventually they gelled together, cricket being the bonding material.

The April wind backs around to blow gently from the south. The sun now has warmth, so much so that some of the men are working in shirtsleeves. Walking across the pea ground, the clag has gone, not even a small lump of soil sticks to your boots. The trailers, loaded for days with seed and fertiliser, are hauled out onto the fields, un-sheeted – and sowing begins. The drills are backed up to the trailers, seed spills from the bags into the hoppers and the first passes are made. Seeding rates are checked, some adjustments made. Within the hour, thirty acres are sown, fertilised and rolled in. The remaining two hundred-odd acres are finished in forty-eight hours, working through the night.

It is important that none of the seed is left lying on the surface of the field. Pigeons have the ability, I'm certain, to inform their chums that peas are being sown and pigeons love peas. To this end hides are now put up, camouflage netting in strategic places. On one side of the pea ground there is a wind break of Japanese larch, mature trees; on another side, lining a driveway, is a row of sweet chestnut, ancient and huge. Pole positions are two massive oak trees, once in a hedgerow long since gone, stuck in the middle of two hundred and fifty acres. These are 'sitty trees' in the local parlance and pigeon gravitate to them because of their exposed position. The birds can see danger coming from a long way off.

The cuckoo arrives this month, timing his visit to match the immigrant warblers and pippets; though here in this part of Hampshire the cuckoo is heard only fleetingly. The estuary topography is not to the bird's liking, seemingly. Ten miles up the road, the cuckoo calls from early morning till dusk. In the enclosure areas of the New Forest, where visitors rarely explore, to hear the cuckoo at first light, echoing hollowly in the deep woodland, is to hear it at its best. The same, but more so, applies to the blackbird. Why it sounds so different in deep woodland I have no idea. To have the privilege of hearing a blackbird singing at dawn in mature beech woodland – which has the acoustics of a cathedral – is to hear the beauty of all nature. It is the same if your horse's metal shoe strikes a stone in woodland. It sounds hollow and ringing, mystical somehow.

The deep woodlands of the New Forest, called 'enclosures', are fenced-off areas of mainly older vegetation and growth. They have names; some plain, some prosaic. Busketts, Pondhead, Denny is just three. If you walk just on the rides you miss so much: walk into the trees, follow the deer paths quietly, walk slowly. What you will see will amaze and delight because you will be alone, apart from the birds and animals. The trippers, campers, grockles, visitors, 'innits', seldom wander from the marked rides or nature trails. If they do, they hardly ever wander more that a gunshot away from where the Forestry Commission would like you to be.

Having spent my younger years studying wildlife from the back of a horse, I can thoroughly recommend it. The birds and animals tend to ignore a passing horse. They seem to pause in what they are doing, and watch you.

There is always the problem of what to do when you see a bird species considered rare; take care whom you tell. If the sighting of a rare bird comes to the ears of the bird police, they will surely disturb them, photographing, ringing the young… then wonder why they disappear.

There was, each year, a small colony of birds we called Cuckoo's Mates. They turned up at the same time as the cuckoo, hence the name. They were also called Snake Birds, as they hissed at you if you went near their nest. In fact, they were wrynecks, the fourth woodpecker, smallish and about the size of the lesser-spotted woodpecker. Beautifully camouflaged to suit living in oak woods, they were fairly rare visitors and almost never nested here. Fellow naturalists kept an eye on them but stayed very quiet about where they were and where they nested.

Growing up, and a career, got in the way of my interest and eventually I rather forgot about them. After a gap of some years, I met a friend in the John Barleycorn at Cadnam and, asking him if the wrynecks still nested locally, his answer said it all: the RSPB found out about them and interfered, so they didn't turn up again that next year. I never saw them again.
It is when the homecoming osprey on their way north are seen fishing on Hatchet Pond that you know shortly you will be listening to the song of the nightingale.

I can count myself lucky to have lived next door to a very large shooting estate: the sort of establishment hated by most of the media because they do not understand what good they do. There were up to eight gamekeepers, old-fashioned by today's way of doing things and, because of these men, there were myriads of songbirds. Such men were naturalists who understood the need for balance, the need to keep predators in check. They knew the ways of wildlife intimately and their passing matches the passing of the song birds and the passing of the nightingale.

But we were privileged to hear the nightingale, to lean on a woodland gate in the half dark and wonder at the volume and tonal richness of this tiny bird's song. Complex in its make-up, short phrases, varied with long single notes, every bird slightly different yet all beautiful.
Who has the best song: the blackbird or the nightingale? Should we add the song thrush to this equation? Or even the tiny wren? Smaller than the nightingale by a good bit, it has a song as pure, loud and wonderful as any, but poets seldom write about poor Jenny Wren.

The National Institute for Agricultural Botany is an organisation that backs up, guides, and shows in seed trials the best of plant breeding. If a farmer needs to know what variety of milling wheat suits his soil type, area rainfall and rotation, he would consult the NIAB list on milling wheat. For generations, plant breeders have tried to improve yields, and succeeded, by crossing strains, breeding new ones and charting their gradual breakdown to leaf and stem disease. It is the same with the world's most important crop. Grass.

Directly after the Second World War, the breeding station at Aberystwyth, mainly concerned with grasses, produced a grass labelled S22. All their grasses were given a number prefixed by the letter S. This grass was a ryegrass, particularly bred for a short-term ley, in this case one year. Drilled in or spun on in the autumn, the grass came early in the spring – too early for some farms, where the land was still wet from the winter's rain for 'get on' (letting the cattle graze). If the cattle were let on to graze it while the land was too wet, the ground would become 'poached': turned into a mud bath, where the cloven hooves of the cattle sink in.
The grass would struggle to survive and certainly, a second cut or graze would suffer. The S22 ryegrass yielded as nothing had

before, half a yard or more tall, great wide dark green leaves, growing so thickly the finger and plate mowers of those days had a job to cope with the crop.

It was very much thought that with the appliance of a little science, the feeding and breeding of grass could be much improved and a more accurate system could be developed. Special leys for special circumstances and farmers were told by the Ministry that if your milk yield went up when your cows went out to grass for the first time in the spring, you were feeding them inaccurately in the winter.

In theory, there could be no gainsaying that; surely, we proudly achieved this. The new grasses, the applied science, we had this milk production properly wrapped up. However, as these bred grasses approached their theoretical perfection, one herd of our dairy cows were always moved to the water meadows, because the bred grasses were being cut for silage and hay. The idea was that you can only make first-class forage from first-class grass and we were an autumn calving herd. Our winter forage needed to be the very best. However, what was left out of the scientific equation was how much the Feel Good Factor of the cows themselves mattered.

After morning milking, on the day the cows were to start grazing the water meadows, the gates into the grazing leys were shut. It was amusing to see their reaction as they wandered down the lane towards them. The first calf heifers, who had joined the herd the previous autumn, looked perplexed as their older sisters became instantly excited by the closed gates. They began hurrying down the lane, getting faster and faster, their pendulous udders swaying wildly from side to side, their memories refreshed; some began to trot, bellowing their excitement.

There was a bridge over the river, but the older animals used to charge through the water, up the opposite bank and into the lush meadows. Here they just frolicked about, kicking up their heels, play fighting with each other and charging at phantoms; then they settled down to eat. The grass in the water meadows was Ancient Pasture, last ploughed, according to the records, during the reign of the first Elizabeth. Most of the actual sward was made up of weed grasses, fescues, bents, rough stalked meadow grass and other Agrostis. There were flowers – cranesbill, milkmaids, buttercups, daisies, dandelion, plantains, tall foxgloves, around the field margins and far too many species to remember or write down.

Deep down, against alluvial earth, a species of white clover grew: its stems like a network of lace, the tiny white flowers barely big enough to see. Through this tracery of stems, tiny stalks of timothy grew, never reaching more than three or four inches high, surviving no doubt on the nitrogen-fixing ability of the clover roots. Another grass grew here in larger patches: sweet vernalls. This made for the most aromatic hay, mingled with other grasses and flowers. When a bale was opened in the winter, the smell of the summer meadows caught sweetly in the back of your throat. The animals loved this hay; the laboratory pronounced it to be as nutritional as a cardboard box, a lot less than barley, straw even.

However, every year as soon as the dairy cows moved onto the ancient swards of the water meadows, the milk went up by as much as sixty gallons per day. Not much per animal, maybe a little over a couple of pints, but up it went on grass that was, on analysis, very poor. The milk quality also shot up, the butter fat content rose generally by more than half a percent, and the 'solids not fat' by more. The milk colour improved, hundreds of pounds were spent trying to get to the bottom of the anomaly – soil testing, testing the nutritional level of each species growing on the meadows, mineral levels were pored over – until in the end we assumed the rise in milk was down to the cows, who just liked being there.

Every year, perhaps the last week in June or the first week in July, an area of the meadows which had been shut to the dairy cows, was cut for hay: a late crop, which, if the sun shone, was quickly made and gathered in. Perhaps the most evocative of smells came from this. The water carriers divided the meadows into long narrow lands, each about fifty yards wide. The soil was not to be compacted, so this haymaking was done using old, light small machinery.

The tractors and the baler engines ran on TVO (tractor vaporising oil). TVO is a type of oily paraffin, which when burnt in an internal combustion engine, smells absolutely wonderful, mixed with the heady smells of the making hay. That heavy scent of sun-drying grass, coupled with the wild flower smell of the meadows themselves, to me is the smell of my home, still deeply loved.

As a child, it seemed never to be dark in the summer; it was called Double Summertime. To me it never mattered what it was called or what it meant; it was just a clever way of extending the hours of daylight.

The grasses in the water meadows were never very tall. There was the occasional tussock of cocksfoot, but in the main it never grew above six to eight inches high. When cut, it dried very quickly, making hay in a very short time. In fact, in a hot summer it became over dry. This caused a problem with the ram balers of the day, so the grass was usually baled in the evening when the dew had come down. The moisture was enough to stick the short grass together, much like putting tap water on one's hair, so that when the baler ram packed it into kerfs, they hung together tightly.

Going to bed in the daylight always seemed like punishment

to me, but it had its compensations. Lying in bed with the windows flung wide, the smell of the making hay would fill the room with its summer fragrance, heady and soporific. The regular beat of the balers' ram, almost like the pendulum of the grandfather clock downstairs, would lull me into deep perfumed sleep.

Long before sunrise, the grey light of the coming dawn enters the bedroom. The sound of the dairyman's dogs barking floats in with the light, along with the calling of the dairy cows as they make their way from the water meadows to their milking parlour. Already the moorhens are up and arguing about the day, splashing and squawking in the feeder stream that borders the garden.

In the village the cockerels who live with their hens in the cottage gardens begin to crow, all different, all recognisable. Mrs Dunn has a light Sussex, a fowl bass baritone, whilst Mrs Darmady has a Wynedot, a weedy creature, whose crow is high pitched and rather feminine. Mrs Rolfe, who knows a thing or two about fowl, has North Holland Blues, great grey-blue birds. Her cock bird, when he deigns to rise, crows loud and deep, quelling the others to silence. He stalks about the village street, attacking cats and terrifying children.

The dawn chorus begins with either the tiny wren or the mistle thrush; the blackbird soon joins followed by the song thrush. After half an hour it becomes difficult to isolate the various bird songs and the air is filled with their singing. The swallows swoop around the yard, hawking at flies above the warm stable muckheap; it is time to get up.

Outside in the yard the air is chilly; the bird song is now wall to wall. All around, even the house martins are up, swooping low to the ground. Looking at the western horizon gives you the reason why. Grey clouds are billowing up and an area of low pressure is developing. The martins, more sensitive than the swallows to this, have followed the insects down with the sinking air pressure. They begin taunting one of the yard cats, chittering at it, as they swoop as close as they dare, missing its head by less than a foot. Leaving the muck-heap wall, the cat makes its way towards the stables with as much dignity as surrendering to the martins is allowed. Which isn't much, as the martins, emboldened now, dive ever closer.

Two hours of walking through the cereal crops looking to spot any diseases is as good a way to start the day as any. In passing, several coloured stakes have been driven into the ground. These are to show where the peewits[*2] are nesting. The stakes are driven into the ground ten yards due south of the nests. This morning, nine stakes were used which makes a total of forty-two this year. They nest mainly on the damper ground, closer to the river, their pitiful cries, as you pass, tugging at your feelings. They are beautiful birds with their iridescent greens and blacks. Their white underparts flash in the light as they wheel and tumble overhead. They soon get used to the people who live here. They rise and swoop about, their broad wings singing in the air, but settle down again immediately the human has passed.

The nest itself is but a scrape in the ground; there may be some grass lining it but as often as not, none. The eggs are a dun colour with darker splodges; pear-shaped and looking too large for the size of the bird. The larger eggs and the food that is in them allow the hatchlings to be strong enough to move about freely and quickly, even before the soft down they are covered with has dried. Closer to hatching date, the male will pitch on the ground and pretend injury, hoping you will try and catch him. You won't, but he will bravely draw you away from where his mate sits tightly on the eggs. They are beautiful creatures, peewits, with their magnificent colours and wonderful aerobatics.

They used to figure frequently on the menu of country homes.

It is no longer done now. I know of no one who would shoot a peewit. When I was a child I thought nothing of eating them and curlew in season. They were both delicious. Woodcock, I think, are the best of wild food, or any food in fact. Wholly wonderful, I haven't shot one of them for maybe ten or a dozen years. Like quail, there are years when the woods and drains are full of them, this year being one. We have a small, south-facing wood on our Devon home. It lays a little wet; I watched just before the snow came this Christmas, and saw dozens dropping in to feed in the moonlight. I am not for one moment saying they should not be shot. In fact, I would suggest it was a dreadful waste not to. It's just that I no longer want to.

Country people view a good fall of woodcock as a harvest to be harvested. I don't suppose two percent of immigrants get shot. Nature cruelly takes a vast toll of woodcock in some years. In 1965, on patrol in the North Sea, heading north up the east coast, we came across a great raft of dead woodcock, floating like dead leaves on the sea's surface. There were hundreds of them. I assumed they were on their way back to Russia and Scandinavia. Maybe they were caught in a squall, I didn't know, but it has been reported to have happened again since.

I no longer shoot them because I am not going to miss. Sport should be challenging for if it is not, then it's boring. A gun is a management tool for me; I shoot vermin, magpies, crows, squirrels, things which damage the balance, predators which kill our ever-diminishing song birds. Woodpigeons have to be shot because of the damage they do to food crops though I shoot woodpigeons also because they are a challenge. They are the cream of shooting. Roost shooting on a windy day tests any shooter.

To have any success at roost shooting, you will have to spend some time watching your quarry; study what they eat at different times of the year. Laid wheat in July, wheat that has gone down flat through wind or heavy rain; Spring barley sowings through February, March and April; oilseed rape as it begins to shoot in the spring. If the summer is hot and dry, pigeons feeding on laid wheat or barley need to drink and, in that case, isolated cattle drinking trough can be productive. Pigeons roost in the daytime as well as night. During the day they will roost in oaks and ash, in the open so that they can see danger approaching. They are very wary and will see the slightest movement; an uncovered white human face they will see half a mile away.

At night, where possible, they will roost en masse in conifer woods and, if not conifer, then deep inside the woods of deciduous trees. To see pigeons flying into these latter woods is to see probably the most agile flyer this country has. The hawks and falcons, the darlings of the bird police, cannot hold a candle to a fit woodpigeon as they jink and slip sideways down into trees.

Shot pigeons are by no means wasted. Country people eat them, and, for a little while, the Sunday glossies featured them in their cooking sections, but they never really caught on. There is an awful ignorance about cooking game in this country, the usual excuse being that when prepared it presents itself as very dry. The other excuse is that a modern urban housewife, mainly, cannot bear the thought of anything being shot. They are right up to speed with fashion there then. Most animals are slaughtered by the Halal method these days. There's not much shooting.

Today's woodpigeon harvest is processed in various gamedealer's small factories and sent tray-wrapped and oven ready to Rungis meat market in Paris from where it is distributed across Europe. Woodpigeons are wild, free as the wind. They live on clover leaves, milky wheat, ivy berries, the best of vegetable greens up on the Fens, berries from the hedgerows. Does any of this matter? Do the urban dwellers need to know how to use basic ingredients? Do they need to know that potatoes, for example, are something more that Aunt Bessie's Roast, precooked in plastic bags?

Probably not, provided there are potatoes enough for everyone and an infrastructure to deliver them to where they are needed at a price that people can afford. If these things are not in place, it might well be a different story.

**

When the first brown trout arrives in the kitchen resplendent in its spring colours, fully mended from its spawning, or a grass snake is seen swimming in one of the slacks of the bends on the river tracking frogs, silage making cannot be far away. Silage is the end product of grass being ensiled in a silo. The grass is cut when the individual grass plants are fully in leaf, left to wilt slightly so as to lose some of the juice and then clamped in an air-tight, or almost air-tight, stack. In the 1950s we cut the grass and buck-raked it into a wedge-shaped clamp which was then covered with a layer of ground chalk. In the winter, it was cut out in great chunks and lifted out with a fore-loader.

Then the layer of chalk was removed with prongs, enough to uncover a week's needs of the cattle. The ensiled grass was then sliced with a hay-knife and pronged onto the feed wagons. This was a daily task, seven days a week, which made it drudgery. Forty years on, there is no back-breaking slog in foul weather, tractors stuck in mud and hands numb with cold.

Today, silage making is an almost clinical exercise. At eight in the morning there is a field of grass, by eight that same evening, the grass is cut, wrapped and safe, stacked in huge round bales at the field side.

Such progress is lacking in many industries, outside of agriculture, because rural people have more application than their urban cousins, or maybe it is a wider breadth of vision.
We have a tractor in the barn, which is fifty-nine years old, a little grey 'Fergie'. It has a saloon car engine, the same as a Standard

Vanguard; the compression ratio is about five to one and that allows it to burn a type of paraffin. The engine is started with petrol and when hot enough, is switched to paraffin. It is about twenty horsepower. We keep it to remind ourselves of how far agriculture has progressed, despite constant meddling by government.

It looks tiny now, hardly bigger than the garden tractor, but its invention by Harry Ferguson was, and is, as important as the invention of the internal combustion engine. Now, the tractor parked outside is 200 horsepower, a great beast of a thing, snorting with its huge super-charged diesel engine. Tractors like these and the complicated machines they power are capable of doing the work of ten little Fergusons. The principles of good husbandry still apply, but today's equipment makes it all so much easier. It has its downside though: there are not the people working on the farms these days. This farm employed twenty-seven men at the end of the Second World War. Now it employs eight, five of whom are employed with the dairy herds. Twice during the farming year contractors come in to help, firstly to clear the cattle yards of their winter accumulation of muck, and secondly the autumn sowing.

This year is Year Seven in this farm's seven-year cycle, so this year is the year that Thousand Headed Kale is drilled into a field named Brain's End. It is ninety acres in total. The field is shaped like a boomerang, skirts the edge of one of next door's main pheasant driving woods. To sow kale here then could almost be construed as a declaration of war. The pheasants are sure to leak out of the woods into the kale, especially on dry sunny days.

Once these pheasants cross from next door to our farm, they change ownership. On our land, they belong to us and this despite the cost of rearing them falling onto next door. This is because they are wild birds. If they were chickens, they would still belong to next door, because they would be domestic stock.

The pheasants are not really any bother to us, except they have different Salmonella pathogens than our farm. The problem with Coccidiosis is taken care of in the pheasant's feed.

By the time the pheasants go to the woods, the kale is just about tall enough to give them some cover. By August they become invisible under the green canopy. The under-keepers keep them from straying too far by 'dogging back' perhaps twice daily: keeping them within an area and getting them used to flying back to the home pen.

The rain that has been threatening for the past few days eventually arrives. The short, sharp scuddy showers which are April have passed along the coastline or gone north of the farm. Now it is our turn. The raindrops are huge, great dollops of beautiful tepid water. The recently tilled pea fields suck it down around the wrinkled green seed, swelling it until each pea is round and smooth. Very soon now, three or four days at most, the miracle of germination will take place; a tiny white shoot will emerge from the two cotyledons.

This is the first root, soon diving down into the fertile soil. Then another shoot shows itself, more delicate than the root pushing up, reaching the light. The tip unfolds into two pale green leaves which turn a darker green as the sunshine caresses the chlorophyll in them. Two days later they well are above the soil's surface, bright green lines stretching away to the crest of the rise.

A new departure for this farm, peas were initially grown to widen the rotation and fill a harvesting gap between the cutting of winter-sown wheat and spring-sown milling wheat, in the autumn. Being something of a new crop to the area, the farm was very much under the microscope, so the project had to at least show some profit. From the outset we knew that woodpigeons would be a problem. The oilseed rape growers fought a continual battle with them and barely won. We tried a fairly radical approach in that we charged the shooters to come and shoot. Against that, we supplied the ammunition and food, sandwiches at lunchtime and dinner in the evening when the pigeons went to roost. We would also keep the shot pigeons to sell to the lady game dealer. Vicki would pick up every evening to make certain the birds were kept as fresh as possible.

How do pigeons, or for that matter any bird species, communicate with each other? How do birds on fields up at Andover find out that there are two big fields of their favourite food at Romsey? A farmer, at Chilbolton, telephoned to say he knew the peas were up because every pigeon in Hampshire and Wiltshire was heading our way. They were waiting, just as I was. They seemed to know right to the day. One pigeon flew slowly along the Japanese larch windbreak, then swung out to cross Lydgate's field diagonally. The pigeon was in no hurry. It slipstreamed from side to side, inspecting the crop, before pitching down and beginning to feed.

Telephone calls were made; ammunition was put out in the hides; the next day, six guns arrived. That day the bag was about two hundred, the next day over six hundred, some of which were feral pigeons from Southampton. The following day, the proportion of feral pigeons was greater, increased by something over two hundred. This carnage went on for days. The fields and hedgerows were festooned in fluffy grey and white feathers, then as suddenly as the pigeons had begun to 'flight' into the peas, they stopped. On the last day there were several thousand birds trying to get at the peas then, suddenly, none. The birds were not hungry, in splendid condition, plump creatures which looked superb plucked and tray-wrapped. They would sell well in France.

The last evening, with the pigeon shooters to dinner, was a noisy affair. They were all retired men from various professions: two vets, two doctors, one vicar, one barrister, one funeral director and two who had worked in the City. Until that week they had not known each other. Now they were firm friends, clamouring to be put at the head of the list should we require pigeon shooters again. This would most probably be after the peas were cut – the combine harvester would lose at least some of the peas in the thrashing and pigeons would most probably come back for these.

The peas that came over the back of the combined harvester are lost to the total crop, so it seems pretty mean to shoot the pigeons at this stage, just for picking up the peas that would go to waste. This opportunity to bring their numbers down should not be missed, however. This year's crop of squabs will have effectively doubled their numbers. It may seem harsh – in fact it is harsh – that these beautiful birds have to be shot in these numbers, but shot they must be. They do enormous damage to farm crops, damage that cannot be ignored.

***

The hedgerows taste of rural England, a taste now forgotten by the urban dweller. A government report I saw stated that most people now were at least five generations away from their rural roots. I rather took this to mean five generations had gone since the urban people had forsaken the countryside for the town. In five generations they have evolved into almost a new species: few know where their food comes from beyond Tesco.

April: so long in coming; so quickly gone. It is the first month when rain falls warm and if it hits your shirt-covered back, you do not gasp with the cold. By April, I am sick to death of ice, frost, snow, and hard-driven cold rain, which both you and the animals turn their backs to and wait its passing, shivering.

Now, in the last week of April, look back and see what changes have been wrought by a few degrees of warmth and more daylight. The river's edge is now marked out by the spear-like leaves of the yellow flag iris. The starwort, now grown and swaying in the current, will soon have its yellow and white flowers, looking like a bridal train of finest lace, belonging to a royal princess.

Creep gently down to the bend below the bridge, stare quietly down into the depths, there is a community down in the deep clear water. The first of the crayfish are beginning to crawl across the bottom, keeping close to the comfort of the bank, evading the eyes of the big trout that sometimes rest from the current here. The grayling that usually ride the currents at the bend's tail are missing. It is their spawning time. Despite being game fish they are classed as a coarse fish because they spawn in the spring. They are proof that the river is clean, free from pollution; trout will stand a degree of pollution, grayling none. They love the fast-flowing stream water, full of oxygen, cold and clear. There is nothing 'coarse' about them; they are very sporting fish and good to eat, should you choose to kill one: just a very gentle fry in butter.

It is strange in that I love angling, but rarely eat fish. The two fish from the river I eat are both classed as 'coarse', grayling and perch. Grayling are said to taste of thyme, I have never found it so. Their flesh is sweet, pink and firm. Perch from a river are the same. Gut them, leave their heads on, put some thyme or rosemary in the cavity, then bake in a covered dish in butter. In both cases, serve with new potatoes and garden peas.

***

January and February, they seem to drag on forever. April passes in the twinkling of an eye. The skylarks that live and breed in the water meadows start our days now. Their songs come down from pale-blue dawn skies. The song itself doesn't have much structure or tonal sweeps, but because it is long, constant and delivered throughout the day, it is not a song that gets ignored. It is a bird wholly of the pastoral areas in this country. I have looked for, but never found, one in the great parks of London. Richmond Park should surely secretly introduce them, but I doubt their song could be heard above the traffic, or Heathrow.

These days to see and hear skylarks in profusion, you have to be away from badger country. They hoover up the nests for a pastime. My favourite places are Pewsey and Uffington. Climb up to the Uffington White Horse before dawn from April till July. They are still there in numbers and you hear more of their song, louder from this standpoint as they start below you. Climb past the high point of the chalk-carved horse and carry on to several hundred feet above the crown of the hill, singing all the way.

The pre-dawn light plays tricks with your vision, making objects more two dimensional. A tired mind looking at a single shrub of hawthorn can make anything of it. A horse maybe, or a dragon or even a man from pre-history; come to give the White Horse some maintenance. That is a daze over his shoulder, surely?

This cold light can help on occasion. I remember being in one of the bottom pools of the river, the first one up from tidal influence. I was setting up my rod, half asleep at four in the morning. I glanced at the water, flat and so clear because there was no glare and saw three sea trout, great big fish. Why they did not see me I will never know. My fingers began to tremble as I tied on the fly, ready. I cast above the trio… the leader and fly hit the water with a hefty splash. Coiled, the leader was a series of loops, supporting the fly just below the surface.

There was nothing I could do except let the tangled mass drift back down the current towards me. I could not mend the fly line into any sort of order without disturbing the fish more than my bad cast had already done.
The leader, fly and the line point were looking ever more of an entanglement. At this point, the middle-size fish turned, cut back down the current brushing aside the tangle of line and slashed at the fly in passing, then dived to the bottom of the pool. I had absolutely nothing to do with it as the fish had

hooked himself in the 'scissors'. This I could see as he fled past my wellingtons, heading for Ocean Terminal in the docks.

The fish fought valiantly for its freedom, taking me two hundred yards downstream from where it had been hooked. Some fish sulk, some fish fly about the river with no idea how best to get away. This one knew every trick in the book. When he began to tire, I decided that he should have his freedom, dropped the rod tip and gave him a slack line, hoping he would throw the hook.

When that didn't work, I guided him into a tiny rill, held him in the net, removed the hook with the forceps and then waited. Gradually he began to recover; still in the net I got him on an even keel, watching as the gill filaments became crimson. Gradually, so as not to startle the fish, the landing net was lowered away from him. The fish was now free. It backed itself to where the rill dropped into the main river, hovering there for a few minutes, backed into the press of water of the river, rising and falling, before effortlessly slipping upstream into the depths. By the time I had walked up to where the fish had taken the fly the sun was up, casting a glare on the surface. If the sea trout was back with his two companions, I could not see. I rather hoped he was. It would be honours even.

CHAPTER FIVE
(May)

May and the fields laid up for hay look promising. The grass crops for hay come from the longer leys of bred grasses on this farm. To the casual observer laid-up fields look much the same as any other field of grass. Look closer, isn't it a little higher in the sward? There is a careful balancing act. Certainly the heavier the crop the better, because it has to not just feed the two dairy herds, the hay has to produce milk as well. The balancing act is getting quality hay as well as lots of it – easy in theory, cut it before it comes 'to head'.

In other words, cut it before the grass plants go to seed, while the grass stem has lots of leaves attached and the weather set fair. Country people have had to re-learn weather forecasting skills as practically everything we do outside is weather governed: to rely on the Met. Office for forecasting these days would be folly.

Haymaking, like other branches of farming, has had several revolutionary methods introduced; we have come from men with scythes to today's Turbo Mowers in less than two generations. Crimpers, wafflers, rollovers, turners, spreaders, row-rakes – the list of hay-making machinery seems endless, until the Acrobat arrived, which was able to do everything – just by changing the configuration of its vast spring wheels.

Hayricks, haystacks, haycocks – these are different words used to describe loose hay collected in a big square or round compacted heap, usually with a sloped roof or, failing this, sheeted down with heavy tarpaulins to keep the weather out. Haycocks, in the north of the country, were smaller haystacks generally raised from ground level by staddle stones, crossed with wooden frames.

Now, most hay is baled; that is, compressed into manageable elongated cubes and tied in shape, with the famous baler twine, without which the countryside could not function. Baler twine is red or blue plastic string that seems to be used for everything: tying around your middle to keep an errant overcoat from flapping in the wind; holding down hedge laying to the pleaches; tying a gate shut; helping a calf into the world and, the funniest thing of all, there is never a length around when you need it most.

Most bales these days are round, great green slices from a green Swiss roll, tied with string and net, each one weighing in at something close to half a ton. Each one of these equates to about twenty of the bales from a pick-up square baler. Clearing a field of hay takes no time now.

***

It is the month to watch the weather and practise your forecasts. Watch and record, get to know your local weather, because mainly it is local. Let me explain that. When an Atlantic front is heading our way, we note where the centre of the low pressure is moving. We know here, for example, that if the low pressure comes ashore say west of Lyme Regis on a south-west wind, we are going to catch just the edge of the weather. If the front comes in much east of this, we are going to have more than enough of it, but it will be through by lunchtime.

'Rain before seven, fine by eleven.' holds good in this area. Except when the low comes up the English Channel, then you are going to have all of it. The storms somehow get stuck at the mouth of the Solent and then it can rain for days.
Knowing your local weather is very advantageous. You can prepare for the worst or spot four or five days of fine weather coming so you can confidently start haymaking.

Poets and painters used to, and still do to a degree, wax lyrical or paint pictures of haymaking. Horses, pretty, beautifully built country girls in poke bonnets, the heady smell of sun-dried grass, the patient stoicism of the sweating horses. Poetic licence, artistic licence; the reality was and is somewhat different. In the days of mowing gangs with scythes going out to mow hay, the day would start generally around half-past three in the morning. This carried on the same when finger and plate mowers were used, pulled by horses. The reason was so that the dampness of the grass could wet the swinging scythe blade, to lubricate its passing through the grass. Pulling a finger and plate mower was very hard work for horses and mowing at half-past three in the morning was cooler for them. There would be fewer flies to pester them and the grass juice and the dew would let the knife slide across the mower deck easier.

Up until the Ferguson arrived, mowers, the machine, had been trailed, pulled by horses, or adapted latterly to be pulled by tractors. I can well remember the great heavy, red and cream machines by Ransomes. They had to be heavy. The 'drive' was from a pair of cast-iron ground wheels from whose turning machine, cut grass passed through a crown wheel gear. They were slow, heavy but infallible and they remained popular until the mid-1960s.

A 'mounted' mower is, as the name suggests, mounted on the three-point linkage and driven not by a land wheel, but by the tractor's 'power take off'. They were fast, very efficient, height adjustable from the tractor's seat and didn't really need the dampness that the other mowers did. It didn't make any difference. For a little while we thought the half-past three start was a thing of the past and it was, I suppose.

We now started after the 'dew had come down', so that by the time of the normal three-thirty start, we had been mowing for six hours!

Cutting grass for hay has its problems. It is later than silage and happens just as the roe deer begin dropping their kids. The game flushers on the front ends of the mowing tractors – chains with weights that are set well out in front of the cutters – shift most of them out of the way. The tractor lights do the same. It gives everything the chance to get away from the chattering blades. Most of the ground-nesting birds don't like the thickness of the crops as it hinders their escape from predators so they tend to nest in the water meadows, away from the rush and tear of modern farming.

The grass lies in long straight lines called swathes, the butt ends sit proud on the stubble, yellow and sickly looking. This happens when the light cannot penetrate down into the sward, because of the thickness of the crop. The stubbles themselves are pale and show between the rows, where the swathe board has placed it.

In the pre-dawn light the field looks as though it is covered with an eiderdown and already the starlings have found these gaps and feed voraciously on the disoriented insects, seeking shelter in the stubbles. Left 'in the swathe' the grass is fairly safe, a light shower will do little harm, so it is a brave man or a man confident in weather lore that chooses now to 'break the swathe' and spread the hay evenly over the field. It will dry more quickly spread, but should the weather turn catchy it will take more harm and lose more leaf, as it will have to be moved more to dry it.

Let us assume that the 'glass is set fair' and the grass *has* been spread. In the 1960s the aim was for 'twenty-four-hour hay': grass cut, dried and baled within a day so as to keep the nutritional value, the leaf to stem ratio high. As the sun comes up, the spread grass looks like a rumpled bed sheet, untidy, haphazard. With the sun's warmth on it, the scent becomes stupefying and heavy. The air shimmers above the grass and the earth, now exposed through the grass stubble, begins to heat up, radiating warmth into the crop. By teatime the grass will have to be turned over, to let the underneath dry.

Each hour that passes now, provided it remains sunny and warm, makes the crop more valuable. Anxiously we walk through the grass picking it up in handfuls, throwing it in the air, testing its moisture level. When it floats back down from being thrown, we know it is 'making'.

There is nothing to do with it now but wait. Overnight the next hay field is 'knocked down', but this time not spread, rather left in the swathe. Now it becomes a question of man power. If things go right for the first field cut, tomorrow it will require the work of eight men, from before tea to supper time. As soon as the sun comes up, the half-dried grass will be 'fluffed up', so the dew is driven out of it. Now it looks much like pale green cotton wool, laid out in rows and any wind now moves it, showing how close to being 'made' it is. Around the outside of the field, the two outer rows are taking longer to dry and the hedges shelter the hay from the drying breeze, casting shadows over the laid grass, denying the sun's warmth.

Agricultural machinery is beautiful in its simplicity and generally over built. There is no scrimping. Why put a half-inch steel bar in place when you have room for a three-quarter inch steel bar? That has always seemed to be the maxim.

A decision before lunch came to the conclusion that the hay in the middle could be baled. The two rows around the outside, still too damp, should be moved out from the hedgerow, using the old side rake, when the rest of the field was cleared. Today, old-fashioned side rakes are seldom seen, pale blue with huge wheels worked from the tractor power take off. They move the swathe sideways, right to left, by about ten feet at each passing, copying the movements of men with wooden hay rakes used for hundreds of years.

The balers, made ready weeks ago for this moment, arrive in the field after lunch; three shiny red machines, serviced, re-belted. They look like new and tested on some straw in the straw yard. They are ready to go. Behind each one, dragging along the ground on metal skids, are the bale sledges, instruments of pain and torture to whoever has to operate them. Basically they were a wooden platform, hinged in the middle, a foot-operated catch allowed the second part to tip about fifteen degrees. The man riding the sledge loaded eight bales on the platform as they emerged from the bale chamber, kicked the release catch and gently, the bottom bales would grip the stubble and slide off, leaving a neat criss-cross of eight bales, ready for the machine to pick them up and put them on the trailer.

The torture involved was that it was continuous, backbreaking, noisy, and very dusty and, being the owner's grandson, I had to do it, quicker and without a stop. There was no favouritism here. That was then, forty years ago, and this is now. With the agricultural workforce ever shrinking, machines have to do much more. The moving of the cut grass happens much the same as it ever did; the small oblong bales of earlier days are now a luxury for the horse hay trade mainly. Smaller farms still use them, lumping them about by hand, but the man on the bale sledge is not heard of now.

There is a nostalgia, almost an industry, built up around how things used to be done. Praise is heaped on old machinery and it is right perhaps to remember and record, to cherish in our minds, the pictures which we remember. The last working horses, dairy cows in magnificent cowsheds, tied in their own stalls: fields of pure-bred cattle, Ayrshire, Jerseys, Guernseys, Shorthorns and the like.

Agriculture is there to produce food. There must also be time and space to show where we have come from and where we are going, surely?

We have "advanced" from one and a half tons of milling wheat per acre, forty years ago, to in excess of three tons. Feed wheat, the wheat that goes into animal feed, is produced at more than four tons per acre. Barley and oat yields have increased commensurately, so much so that we now have a vibrant grain export industry. How has this come about, this wonderful superabundance of grain? It is a huge blessing to be self-sufficient in our staple food. I use the phrase 'self-sufficient' advisedly. It goes with some of the other eco-warrior soundbites: 'sustainability' is another, 'organic' yet another.

If the agricultural lobby had listened to the eco-lobby, none of this would have happened. The higher yields have been achieved by better husbandry, much improved varieties from the plant breeders and what is called artificial fertiliser and agro-chemicals. Agro-chemicals, or 'pesticides' as sections of the media, the BBC and other ignorant urban people wrongly refer to them as, are weed killers and fungicides. Some are specific and some are broad spectrum. The specific are weed killers, used for situations like wild oat or blackgrass infestations: broad spectrum weed killers take out the broad leave weeds in crops. I do not know a single farmer who likes using them, mainly because they cost so much. Believe me, if they could get away without using them, they would.

Weeds lower yields and infect the food crop with their own rusts and fungus so they have to be taken out. Also, a pernicious weed, such as mayweed, when combined, spreads its heads in the grain, making drying and cleaning more difficult. Fungicides are totally innocuous mixtures, probably less potent than dishwasher tablets and certainly less of a problem than birth control pills. Pesticides are for killing pests.

They are not used as prophylactics, only ever as 'spot' action as when used as treatments to rid a crop of aphids. They are expensive mixtures which are only used when needed. And when you see a crop sprayer in a field, why always assume the worst? It could be spraying something as innocuous as sea-weed extract, used to boost trace elements in the soil.

Early May sees the sprayers out, cleaning the arable crops. Every farm's spectrum depends on the rotation used. This farm has a seven-year cycle, the crops grown are cereals, early potatoes, forage crops, short-term leys and longer leys. The muck produced by the dairies, pigs and horses (belonging to the lady who rents the stables) amounts to about two thousand tons. This is all used and none is sold away so the land is always kept in good heart. The main weed problem we have is chickweed, which is not a problem at all as chickweed only grows where the soil is well up together. Its presence becomes almost welcome.

Weed control is an art, an art that changes with the weather pattern. Our Brain's End field, the one this year with a forage crop to be drilled, has grown on nicely after the grass was cut for silage. The grass and weeds are now about six inches high. This will produce a substantial amount of humus-making material. Just as importantly, the weeds, plantains and dandelions will have used lots of their strength in shooting up towards the May sunshine. Now they get ploughed in, put a foot underground by the digger ploughs used on such occasions.

There are lots of different sorts of plough; the differences are in the shape, length and depth of their bodies, the curved blades that turn the soil in and over. A digger plough is the one that ploughs deepest and takes the surface soil down to between a foot and fourteen inches, burying the residual grass and weeds down to where the kale roots will eventually get. Also, the deep ploughing puts the crane-fly grubs and leather jackets down deep where they perish before the kale roots reach that far. Some only survive to be killed by the lime dressing that goes on for the kale. Kale, being a brassica, needs a high ph, an alkali soil, which in turn is good for the spring wheat, which will follow the forage crop.

By this time next year Brain's End will be carrying a dense crop of Sappo spring wheat which will be cut in that autumn and delivered to the flour mill the following year in July. Farming is long term, ordered and, hopefully, will go on forever.

***

A couple of hundred years ago, a friend's family bought a farm near what was the village of Old Basing, Old Basing at the turn of the last century was a pretty village quite close to the market town of Basingstoke. Old Basing still seems a bit like a village. It has had some development: a couple of private housing estates for middle managers who generally work in London, easy by train, or in Basingstoke. Basingstoke feels nothing like a small market town today. It doesn't feel like anything in fact because it exhibits no character or soul. It is the result of planners feasting on emetics. If Tower Hamlets was a mistake then Basingstoke was a bigger one. It sits among the rolling downs of Hampshire like a festering carbuncle.

The people who live in Old Basing, not a couple of gunshots away, hate to be reminded of their bigger ugly sprawling neighbour. They invent ways of convincing themselves that they live in a country village – after all, that's why they left London – even to having a monthly, self-produced village magazine. The farming family, of whom I spoke earlier, having suffered complaints from the new country dweller for years – dung spreading, cows mooing, cocks crowing, harvesting with a combine harvester – now write a monthly column in said village magazine, informing the people of Old Basing what they are doing and why. Complaints turned to interest, interest into practical help. Now almost everybody lives happily together.

Pit villages were there because of coal, initially probably on the surface all around them. Anyhow, it was enough to make somebody think: 'This is perhaps a good place to stop over for a time.' They stayed, mined the coal to sell, more people joined them, more dwellings were built and suddenly there was a community.

It was the same in sparsely populated areas. A chap saw some good land, well watered from a river that was teeming with fish. The land was light and friable, a good place to live perhaps. He noted the high-water mark of the river from previous flooding, built his dwelling above this and settled down to farm. He is no longer a hunter gatherer.

His generation know how to hunt, know how to gather, but now he has a roof over his head. In front of him are fish running up the river; wild fowl for the taking; deer and boar and what he can grow. This is a simplistic description of the beginnings of a 'settlement'. People join in and pretty soon the settlement becomes a hamlet and eventually a village. At what point one becomes the other I have no idea. If you take the settlement of the American frontier towns about the only authentic thing Hollywood get right about them was the blacksmith's shop on Main Street.

For agriculture to have progressed here (and certainly in America) there had to be blacksmiths and wheelwrights – the wheel makers. Equally important were the farriers: men who made all those horse and oxen shoes and fitted them.

Ponder for a moment how a wooden cartwheel is made, the absolute precision required. The hub, generally made from elm, has to have the spokes inserted. This can be as many as sixteen in a showy gig; then the fellows – the rim of the wheel made in sections all fitting so closely that the join is hardly visible. Next, a rim is fitted to the wooden wheel. This is a flat piece of metal, shaped in a perfect circle, welded shut with the blows of a hammer on the rim's molten ends and made to just be a little smaller than the circumference of the wooden wheel.

This steel rim is heated in a pit, expanding it enough to slip over the wooden rim, and then doused in cold water, to contract it. This process draws it into the wooden rim, pulling the various sections of the wheel together tightly, leaving a metal rim to take any wear from the road surface.

The skills of the blacksmiths, wheelwrights and farriers were all specific to the motive power of the day – the horse. The wheelwright may well have attached himself to a wagon works, a place where farm wagons, traps, gigs and the like were made. Both the blacksmith and the farrier might well have attached themselves to a big farm, for the sake of having a building to work in, but as with today, they would seek to maintain their independence.
Now, at home, the forge and wheelwright shops are redundant: the forge remains as it was when it was finished with, the tools carefully stored. The wheelwright's shop is empty, its detritus outside in the yard; the old brick-lined pit where the wheel rims were heated is now a flower bed. On an oak support, there is the lever which pushed the rubber rims into the rails on gig wheels.

The village, built to house some of the farm workers, essentially a gentle crescent of detached three-bedroomed cottages as alike as peas in a pod, now house people who work in Southampton or even London. As the farm's workforce contracted, homes became empty, both on the farm and in the village. Those families left in the village in farm cottages wanted to live within the boundaries of the farm. Southampton, like a cancer, had spread to the estuary, with all the ghastliness that that engendered and far too close for comfort.

Soon there were eight empty cottages in the village belonging to our farm. They were all renovated and the ground floors had extensions. The vicarage had been renovated, with a view to us moving from the main house, but the expense was ever more burdensome, so it never happened. Instead it was let to a medical consultant who liked the idea of living in a grand old house.

When I was very young, one of my duties was to ride down to the marsh and check the cattle that lived there. Variously, dry dairy cows, old dairy cows putting on weight before going to slaughter, or what few beef animals we raised. Then, whenever I went down through the village, it looked alive. There were dogs roaming about, generally some chickens. The gardens looked productive and full of produce or flowers.

These days, the place is empty by eight-thirty in the morning. The people who live there are mostly transient. They mainly come from hospitals in Southampton: doctors, consultants, senior nurses, who rent the houses on short-term leases before buying their own houses once they have decided to settle in.

Southampton was well served with hospitals. There was the General, the Chest Hospital and the Royal South Hants. The people in the village seemed spread between the three. They were friendly approachable people in the main and because they were our tenants, we had to be on call should anything go wrong. It was usually blocked drains.

It was immediately obvious when you fell into conversation with them that their knowledge of things rural was not so much scant as non-existent. Only the one, who seemed in charge of everything, Matron Dewey, knew about birds and could tell the difference between hay and straw or knew what they had come from. Matron Dewey had an almost childlike curiosity about matters rural. She had an absolute passion for tractors old and new and loved nothing quite so much as ploughing and ploughing matches. I once spent a Sunday morning crawling over our combine harvester showing her how it worked.

Penelope, for such was her name, was a very feminine forty-something, blonde with huge powder blue eyes and a brisk, almost sharp manner, which belied the true woman she was. To be in her company was to be surrounded by her wonderful warmth and compassion. We all missed her dreadfully when she moved on to higher things: a professor of nursing who could plough, drive a combine harvester, shoot and cast a fly.

***

It was in 1968 when I last heard the corncrakes calling on the water meadows at home. They had been there in profusion through the '20s and '30s. The Second World War began their rapid decline, despite our efforts after the war to save them. Down below the estuary was considered a 'target-rich environment' by the Germans: the docks in Southampton; the tar distillery in Totton; the Spitfire factory in Eastleigh; the MTB yard at Woolston; Vosper Thorneycroft, to name just some of them.

The Germans, not really known for their sense of humour, were pretty fed up with the Hurricanes and the Spitfires, so they decided to try and kill the 'little planes' at birth by bombing the factory. To counter this, large fires were lit on the water meadows, which the Germans bombed with gusto, but if the Germans are not known for their sense of humour, they are also not known for being stupid.

They came back in the daylight, burnt the tar distillery, bombed the docks, wrecked the Spitfire factory, and strafed the town at random and upset the corncrakes. The water meadows that were bombed were left looking like the Somme battlefield then, later in the war, the meadows became one huge army camp: thousands of Americans waiting to go across to France. Where the corncrakes went in those years is anybody's guess.

There is an old sepia photograph at home of a group of shooters on a bittern shoot at Stanpitt Marsh. Stanpitt Marsh borders Christchurch Harbour, or used to. Now there is a tiny nature reserve sandwiched between a golf course and a suburb called Stanpitt: row upon row of houses. Obviously the bittern have long since departed. I'm told by the ancient sportsman of the day that bittern made good eating and Stanpitt was the place to find them.

There is a suburb of Southampton named Bittern, where again the birds were found in numbers, enough certainly to take an annual harvest or, as it is called today 'sustainably managed'. There is absolutely nothing there to recommend the area, just another ghastly hotchpotch of the much-vaunted multicultural society. No self-respecting bittern would be seen dead there, which brings to mind the story of the King's Somborne bittern.

Found dead on the road between Romsey and Somborne, the bird caused a gentle stir. Those in the know knew the birds had established themselves in the marshes below Stockbridge and had been there for several years, a breakaway colony from the birds living just above Romsey. There are now, and always have been, bittern down in the reed islands of the estuary – unlikely to be heard these days because of the constant noise in the area and their days are disrupted by the constant bright lights of the illuminations of the estuary bridge.

In a way it is the same as Stockbridge Marsh (or Common as it is called): the birds are there but the people who would know them are not. There are not many country people in the beautiful town. It has for the past thirty years been gradually taken over by people from London, now surely a commuter town. Look at the shops and you can see its rural heart stopped beating years ago. These people would hardly know what a bittern is. Probably best in fact if they do not know. They are less likely to be a disturbance to the birds.

It is simply horrible for the native residents of a small market town or large village when estate agents describe a property as being 'in this much sought-after village' or 'in wonderfully unspoilt countryside'. The natives of the 'sought-after village' advertised in a weekend glossy know that their village will be dead within a generation, the houses bought up by town people who only live in the village at weekends. Gradually the shops are unable to survive on just 'weekenders' and close while another village nearby can become a weekend retreat for in-comers, and stay empty during the week, destroyed.

Houses not lived in 'go backwards': deteriorate rather quickly, especially if the houses are not lived in during the winter months. They succumb to damp and fungus or, more extremely, the criminal element. They know their break-in crimes will probably not be discovered for some time, if at all.

***

This winter's kale ground is now being ploughed; the pasture turns over square and firm furrows are held together by the grass roots. There is no great rush to get it done so the opportunity is taken to 'train up' a young tractor driver. This requires three tractors and ploughs, one to go in front of the youngster, one in behind him and the learner's plough has been deliberately badly set up. The tractor in the lead position is usually driven by the head tractor driver, aiming his bonnet at a ranging pole at the far end of the field. His plough seems effortlessly to turn three perfectly square blocks of sod over with not a wisp of grass stubble showing between them. The second tractor stays straight enough, but the rear furrow of his work collapses back into its original position. Gradually, with help from the more experienced men the youngster adjusts his plough so that the earth turns over in symmetric square furrows. There is still grass showing between the slices so, next, he has to master the skim coulters. These are like tiny ploughs that lay against the coulter wheels, taking the corner from the right angle the coulter wheel cuts. Mostly within the hour there are nine perfect furrows cut with each pass of the three tractors. The plough the newly trained ploughman is using will become 'his'. No one but him may use it. When it's fixed to the linkage of 'his' tractor that morning, it's done in a stylised ritual, the heavy red and green plough smelling of new paint and fresh grease, the beams as straight as lasers. By the day's end the young man will be told how much more will be in his pay packet at the end of the week. Now that he can 'set his own plough' and hold his own with the older men.

Held together by the grass roots, the sod turns over and holds its shape; the soil is dark, rich and smells alive. The turned furrows shine gently, the plough bodies having smeared the dampness. They run across the field, arrow straight and uniform. As the sod slips across the plough bodies it seems to hiss as the stones and soil polish them to silver, better than silver maybe.

As they reach the end of each run, the ploughs lift from the earth and wink in the sun as the tractors turn to come back across to where we stand. The short halt for lunch allows quiet to descend. The men sitting on the bank at the edge of the field eat their food with their great dry hands stained with earth, drink their scalding tea from white enamel tin mugs and discuss the shortness of girls' skirts in the town. When there is a gap in the conversation and laughter, the click of contracting metal accompanies their thoughts as their tractors cool. Despite today's luxurious air-conditioned tractor cabs, the men still lunch under a hedge or on a bank, the same as they have done for generations: the smell of the rich turned earth, a dressing on their lunch.

Within the memory of the older men there would have been the smell and company of horses. They too would have been under the hedge having lunch, nosebags stuffed with oats, fresh crushed with apples or whatever their partners could find for them to make their lunches as good as their own.

Out on the furrows the rooks methodically clear them of any grubs and insects. The seagulls are too lazy for this, so they wait, standing on one leg, watching with their soulless yellow eyes, waiting for the humans to continue ploughing.

As they rise as one from lunch, a half-grown leveret springs from the hedge and runs across the plough towards next door's pheasant cover. Disturbed by the men's sudden movement, it gallops half-heartedly down the furrows, the men watching and smiling, remarking on how well grown the young hare is. Smiles fade quickly as they see a large bird of prey in a shallow dive, not fifteen yards behind the young hare.

'Run Marjory, run!'*3

It would be a very close-run thing for the hare, now flattened*4 out and running for her life. It looked too late. There's a shot, the pursuing bird looked as though it had flown into an invisible wall before crashing into the plough. Another, unseen by the watchers, had been approaching at an oblique angle. It soared upwards then collapsed into the fence, to hang flapping weakly. The sound of the second shot reached them before they could speak, a handful of feathers floated on the breeze.

'Well done! Well done!'

The birds were buzzards, the first seen in the area for years, apparently nesting on Southampton Common, a large area on the north of the city covered sparsely in mature trees. What happened was completely right as far as these men were concerned. They had heard about the demise of the brown hare in counties to the west of them, brought about by the buzzards killing the leverets because of the shortage of rabbits.

They were all agreed: Hampshire could do without the buzzards, but the hares are sacrosanct. The dead birds were placed in the next furrow, to be buried on the next pass of the ploughs. The shots had sent the rooks skyward. They circled high above the plough land protesting their innocence to wrongdoing. Soon they had forgotten and fell in behind the tractors again, hundreds of them. What grain rooks take from the drillings, or laid cereal, is more than repaid by the pests they eat. If this day was typical, with perhaps 400 rooks following the ploughs and each consuming 100 slugs or leather jackets each day, it does add up to a lot of pests done away with and a much better crop of kale to come.

With the ploughing finished, the area is lightly disc harrowed, just enough to level it a little, ready for the chalk dressing. Kale is a brassica and it requires the soil to be fairly alkali. The following crop of spring wheat will require the same sort of alkali level. The chalk dressing is as the name suggests, dug from the Downs, crushed and sieved to get granules of about half an inch. Because the land for the kale is light and fairly free draining, the nutrients can leach*5 out fairly quickly.

The sod created with the grass roots hold this up to a degree, but it is something to be aware of. The chalk comes from the chalk pit in ten-ton loads from just a few miles north of the town on four-wheel drive lorries with spreaders on their rears. It is quick and efficient and they are prepared to work to suit the local rush hour, so the town is not blocked with lorries at the wrong time.

Once the chalk has been spread, the disc harrows are used again, this time to proper effect. They cut the sod to an ever-finer tilth, mixing the chalk into the top four inches. The seed is drilled next through a precision drill which spaces the seed accurately to obviate 'singling': seven rows of kale, two rows of swede.

The type of kale we use is called Thousand Headed. It can grow to about four feet in height, which makes it difficult to 'strip graze'. The kale would touch the electric fence wire and short it to earth. The fence is therefore run down through the lines of swede, which rarely reach more than a foot high.

'Strip grazing' is a way to ration the amount of kale that the cattle eat and tread in with their feet: controlling their grazing by a strand of wire with an electric charge running through it (not enough ever to hurt them, just a gentle reminder to stay where they are meant to stay). It works quite well early in the autumn, until the ground gets too wet; the cows then 'poach' it and turn the ground into a sea of mud. Rather than that, the kale is cut and taken to the cows in their yards. The swedes get eaten should the ground get dry enough for the animals to go out again and if it doesn't dry out, some swedes are lifted for the people on the farm and ourselves. The rest are ploughed in, before the spring wheat is drilled into the field. We are not allowed to give them to the hospital or people in the town anymore: 'Elf and Safety mate, yer see.' I don't, but that's the way of it these days. When I see a swede, shrink-wrapped, not covered in earth as it should be, I know the world has turned on its head.

Once the seed is sown all that is left is rolling: such a common thing, rolling. Why do we do it? Not to put pretty patterns on the soil, or great silver stripes in the grassland, I promise. We roll spring-sown crops to conserve the moisture in the soil, also to firm up the seed bed and push the soil around the seed to snug it down ready to grow. We don't roll winter-sown crops because the sown ground surface needs to be fairly 'nobbly' so that when, let's say, the winter wheat germinates, the large clods of earth give the tender plants some shelter. It will settle down tight enough on its own with the rain that is going to fall on it before spring.

With the bulk of the hay harvest gathered for the moment, there was perhaps a little time to take stock, even a little time for oneself. It would soon enough be time for the main annual holidays the men needed to take. There would have to be the usual juggling and filling in for those absent, so there was very little time away for me.

Being up at four-thirty on a wet February morning is not to be recommended: the same cannot be said for being up with the dawn on a late May morning. You can pretend you are alone in the world, selfishly enjoying the dawn.

Romsey is the last town on the river before it reaches the tideway. It never suffered the affront of becoming an 'overspill' area as did Basingstoke and Andover and, as a consequence, still has parts which remind the native of what it once was – a tiny market town with its own soul and lots of small shops to serve a largely rural community. It was, in fact, a comfortable town. Romsey had never suffered the invasion of the *telestocracy* when the BBC arrived in Southampton – the Royal connection with Broadlands was probably not to their taste. The tele people favoured Lyndhurst and went to live there, which was a blessing.

Just upstream from Middlebridge, on the Cadnam road leaving the town, the town mill race empties into the main river: this, the mill race from Town Mill. Just before Middlebridge it runs through the Memorial Park and, as the name implies, it is a place where the fallen of the town are remembered. It is a place of mown grass, flowerbeds and some mature trees. There is a Japanese field gun on a tarmac circle amongst the spring tulips, brought back from the Second World War by Lord Mountbatten.

I like to think that even in the confusion that reigned at the time of the Japanese surrender, Mountbatten thought of his home and the men of Romsey who would not be coming home. Generations of Romsey's children have played on it, but these days it is thought far too dangerous and not really very PC.

Between the park and the back gardens of some houses on the

opposite bank the mill race tumbles over a gravel bed at some considerable speed, or it did at the time I am speaking about. It always defeats me as to why the energy of the river is no longer used. The river is still there doing what it has always done. There was a turbine in Sadlers Mill producing electricity for the Broadlands Estate and once installed, cost nothing much to run. Even if it did not produce electricity enough for all the estate's needs, there was more than enough for the house. These things do not extract water. They just borrow it, pass it through a turbine and it gives you electricity. It doesn't interfere with the migratory fish, so why not keep them running? I do wonder who makes up the rules for what's progress...

Anyway, whilst the mills were running the mill race was good but made for extremely difficult fishing. In the winter there was not a better place in the whole valley for big grayling. In the summer the trout were difficult, but huge. Sometimes a salmon resting would wander into the race, to be tempted by a prawn. It was a fun river that gave up its inhabitants only unwillingly.

In the steely grey light before dawn in May was the most exciting time to be there. If you could see the fish tucked up under the far bank, or hovering in an eddy, you could be sure that they had seen you. That would keep their heads down, ignoring your fly. The angler had to know the stream to catch anything, know every undercut on the bank, any deeper hole on the almost level bed and be able to cast accurately well forward, at least twenty-odd yards. Stand with your back against one of the sycamore trees, so your silhouette doesn't show and watch the stream. Listen to the birds for a few minutes.

Because of the gardens opposite there are dozens and dozens of birds. I don't know where there are more blackbirds than here. They sing against each other in the new light, their rich fluty warble has a quality that no other bird can quite match. Quite close, almost under my feet I can hear the complex song of the dipper. She nests generally in the remains of some roots overhanging the water. It is quite incredible that this tiny bird can plunge into such fast-flowing water and walk along the stream bed looking for food. I'm told the shape of its body with the press of water on it helps it stay submerged. It eats caddis larva, small beetles, shrimps and whatever it can find on the stream bed. Every time I come here, I see a dipper. I doubt it's the same one, but they do tend to stick to maybe a length of stream of one hundred yards.

Only when there is movement on the rooftops of the houses opposite, is there any movement from within the stream. A large brown trout, very thin, hardly 'mended'*[6], hurls itself from the water landing with a great splash, thirty yards upstream. I am certain this particular fish and I are acquainted and if it is the same one, I have hooked him three times. The first time was two Septembers back, he was fully mended, five pounds odd of solid muscle; he bested me with a scorn that seemed palpable on the day. The second time I fooled him with my fly and brought him to my net, beaten.

If you are not going to kill a fish it is probably best not to handle it. In the landing net they will generally lie quietly whilst the hook is removed especially if, like me, you fish with a barbless hook. They are unharmed, but forever wary. The third time I hooked him and brought him to book, I could see when I got him close that he was still a bit skinny from spawning. I gave him some slack line so he could throw the hook. He was away instantly, flying upstream. I certainly didn't want to try for him on this day, rather I would leave him, to mend and fatten up. I would give him a wide berth, not wanting him to see me, to avoid him charging off upstream frightening every fish between the park and Mottisfont.

It may seem an odd place to fish, in a park amongst flowerbeds, with great banks of tulips. Beautifully edged beds, alive already this day with great bumble bees, their deep humming buzz loud in the quiet of sunrise and the first warmth from the sun. The fishing belongs to the town and is let on a day ticket, seven shillings and six pence per day. There are few takers because the water is so difficult to fish with a fly, which is mandatory. Wookey and Wallis, the auctioneers, administer the finance and, being our land agents, it's easy for me to pay up front for ten days of my choosing. That is how it used to work. I don't know now because these days a fish hook is far too lethal a thing to be flying about in a public place, where someone may get accidentally hooked.

Avoiding the old adversary by walking far out into the park was easy. Time is getting on and the first of the farm workers cycles along a footpath heading towards his place of employment. He waves, smiling wryly... he would like to be fishing perhaps.
Another fifty yards upstream, by a sweet chestnut tree, there is what remains of an ancient footbridge, a back way into the Abbey precinct. The ancient stone support jutting into the stream is all that remains now; it causes a small slack eddy, a resting place for a fish. From twenty-five yards it looks nothing, just a patch of water four feet by four feet, not catching any light because of the canopy of the trees.
The fly, a *Coachman* tied on a *Number Twelve Mustad* hook, flew across the distance to the broken bridge support, hit it gently and dropped into the eddy, circled once before the dragging line pulled it into the current. Watch and look hard. Did the water in the eddy wobble? Wobble is an indefinable movement of the water, that only an angler sees.

The second cast lands short and immediately the current drags the fly, enough to frighten the fish maybe. The third cast lands perfectly, even before the fish, which you know instinctively is there, moves to it. You know he is yours. There is a dimple on the surface of the eddy, near where you judge your fly to be, the line tightens; the fish is hooked. For what seems an age, there is an unseemly tug-of-war, nothing more. There is no thrashing, no movement from the tiny patch of water, just a completely locked fly, almost as though caught on the old bridge support. As your mind begins to doubt, the line moves into the current, the pull is directly upstream by something heavy and unstoppable.

What started out as a brisk walking pace, checking the fish, making it pull, soon becomes a helter-skelter untidy gallop, bending rod in one hand, landing net in the other. There is a good maxim here – do not give too much line to an unstoppable fish. A good fly line costs twenty quid; know when you are beaten.

The fish turns and comes powering back downstream. This is pretty unusual; stripping the line back is the only way to stay in contact. There is a heap of white fly line being trampled into the grass as a fairly hefty grilse*[7] rushes past, towing line behind him. Gently checking the line he comes back up, fighting all the way. Line is being gained on the reel, as I move upstream again in a more controlled manner. More confident now, I make him fight me for the line too hard. He flies back downstream again, the reel singing beautifully, myself swearing horribly.

By running the line out so that it bellies out behind him, pulling on the hook the fish moves upstream away from the pull. Three times we did this, gradually the fish began to tire or that was the impression he gave. As I drew him closer, even to the point of laying the landing net under the water ready to enfold him, he rolled on the cast and the hook came away. He didn't power away, he just drifted into the middle of the stream, collected himself then swam gently back to where he had started his day, by the stone bridge support.

This episode was not in any way a disappointment, I promise. Fishing is not just about catching fish to eat or kill. I remember back to this fish which was in the mill race. I don't know why he was there, when he could have been in the main river. Maybe he hatched from his egg in the mill race at that time when the people above the town on the main river, the riparian owners, did not want the salmon above Romsey. They were checked at Sadler's Mill.

Some obviously passed the mill, but not the whole run. They had to spawn somewhere, and a place like the mill race was one of them. Provided the angler does not touch the fish with dry hands, breaking the covering of protective slime, I do not think they suffer harm. The net is of a soft cotton type and big enough to hold an eight-pound fish with ease and since I have always been taught to fish with barbless hooks, once the fish is in the net and the pull of the line relaxes, the hook generally falls out. Sometimes, it may well catch in some cartilage but then I just reach down with a set of artery forceps and lift the hook away, the fish never leaving the water.

Fishing in the park one day I hooked a somewhat smaller grilse, about four pounds in weight. After a short but fierce struggle, I brought him to the net and then let him go. There was a female on a horse watching me who offered me money for the fish, even before it was in the net. When I refused quietly then released it without harm, she was quite offended. It was a long time ago, but I suggested she learnt the skill of fishing with a fly so she could catch her own and appreciate then why I very often released a fish. I wonder now if she did.

Most of my fishing is fly and, as with all field sports, there are rules, which gives the quarry species 'law'*[8]. For example, I could if I so wished break the laws and pull a small spinner up through the mill race and denude it of fish in a week. You would be after all fooling the fish into catching his prey species, a perfectly natural thing to do. It is far too easy, so you don't do it!

Fly fishing is not as difficult as a lot of people would have you believe. In essence you are offering the fish a copy of his natural food, either floating on the surface or with a nymph down at the fish's depth. On the local chalk streams the idea is to spot a feeding fish. Keeping downstream of your chosen quarry, you offer him an artificial fly much like the one he is feeding on; 'upstream dry fly' this is called.

You have to know the flies that come off in a major hatch – everyone knows, for example, the Mayfly. Sometimes the river produces a hatch of these that seem to fill the air, a blizzard of flies. The fish in these circumstances seem to throw caution to the wind and charge about grabbing them, on the water's surface, above in the air, anywhere. These times are known as 'duffer's fortnight' when the trout are very easy to catch, or meant to be. I have never found them so.

Fishing, to the majority of people, conjures up lines of men sheltering behind fixed, large green brollies, staring at a float, with bait suspended beneath it in the water. That sort of fishing is a game of skill and patience and is called Coarse fishing – why, I do not know. There is nothing that is in any way coarse about it. If I started now to describe the equipment these anglers use, I could write a book larger than *War and Peace* and still not get enough words written about it all.

Fly fishing requires a lot less. Generally you carry one rod, two reels, a landing net, some artificial flies, a priest for the last rites and Polaroid glasses. You've already read about fly lines; these are superb nowadays, made of wonderful synthetic materials which cost the earth. There are many types so I will just describe my own, a double-tapered *Number Six Floating: White*. There you are that's clear enough I think! That's what's printed on the box, anyway.

Seriously, the line is white. This does not show on the surface as much as other colours to the fish, or so I think. I have studied the colours, lying on the bottom of the river and looking skyward. The line is thirty yards long, varying in thickness from the middle or belly, towards both ends. In the middle it is probably three millimetres thick, tapering to about one and a half millimetres.

Whipped to each end is a braided loop about half an inch long; one end is attached to the backing on the reel, thin, braided, very strong, light cord. This backing on the reel gives you an extra length of line for playing a heavier fish.

An angler's saying: 'The fish took me right down into the backing.' In other words, the fish was too strong to stop for some time. On the other end, the braided loop is to attach your 'cast' or 'leader': the monofilament length of nylon to which is attached the artificial fly. This cast is tapered from the fly line to the tip. I am lazy, I buy my casts made up with each one beautifully packed in its own envelope. The tip on this leader is so thin you can barely see it and yet it takes a strain of four pounds weight before it snaps. It has to be thin, so the fish cannot see it, but at the same time strong enough to land the fish.

Artificial flies are legion – hundreds, maybe thousands of different sorts and shapes from all over the world. They are far too numerous to list and my advice would be to get local knowledge from the nearest angling shop to where you are going fishing. I have three fly boxes: one for salmon flies; one for trout flies; and one for grayling. As grayling are by far and away my favourite fish, as a quarry and for its sporting beauty, I will just describe the contents of that particular box.

Of proper flies there are *Greenwell's Glory*, *Black Gnat*, *Hare's Ear* and *Coachman*, in varying sizes, both wet and dry flies. Of the nymphs, nymphs being the larval stage of water-hatched flies, I use: *Sawyers Bug*, *Red Tag* and *Pheasant Tail* – and having fished the Frome, the Avon and the Test for most of my life, I have never felt I needed more.

CHAPTER SIX
(June)

At last it is summer, summer proper. It no longer seems to get dark. When I was a child going to bed and sleeping in the daylight seemed like a punishment. Older now and with the sounds of the world outside going to sleep, whilst lying in bed with all the windows wide open, is luxury. The house martins are crammed into their nests up under the eaves, their chittering conversations telling me that they are content. They have spent all of the day swinging on the breeze over the house and stable yards. The swallows, absent in the daytime, have spent their day over the river or over the newly cut grass fields.

Far away, certainly not on this farm, a tractor is working, a background sound you would not hear in the daytime. This evening though, the machine is the only one working. Listen and wonder at the undulating note of the far-away exhaust to know what work is being done. The rasping call of a grey partridge is louder than the tractor's note. The cock bird is calling to the last of his family to join him, where he has chosen to 'jug'*9 this night. From the sound, they are jugged along the driveway leading to the shorthorn dairy, in the rough grass, just out from the spread of the sweet chestnut trees. The first pale light of morning will find them delicately picking up grit from the driveway. The cock and hen and perhaps six to ten youngsters will be busy but alert to things around them. They know the driveway is used by the resident foxes.

The chill of dawn wakes you around four-thirty. Even in this first week of June it feels cold. It isn't really cold, just colder than when you went to sleep some hours ago. The young lady who shares my life and bed has disappeared under the bedclothes, just a lock of red gold hair shows on her pillow, letting me know she is in residence. Outside, the sky is a pale blue-grey and, watching from my bed, I can see wildfowl, hatched early in the year, flying in groups to the estuary.

They have spent the night roosting or feeding on the various rivers and streams, which criss-cross the land on this end of the farm. You know that they are this year's birds, as they still fly in a plump*[10], not 'skeined out'*[11] in their normal V formation.

Downstairs, the hall, still in grey shadow, smells of the summer flowers the room is decorated with. The kitchen is warm, with none of the hint of dampness the house can seem to have at this time of the year. The Aga sits like a square Buddha exuding its year-long warmth, quelling the goose pimples of my still bare legs. The summer daylight arrives as the sun climbs over the ash trees on that side of the garden. There is a single cloud which makes a fleeing shadow over the roofs and walls of the farm buildings, leaving them bright and shiny before the damp of the night is turned into smoky rising vapour by the now warm sun.

***

The mother of the twins who were on their way to being eaten by an urban fox (BBC 2010) was vilified and threatened by people who supported the fox in all of this. Their threats were of the normal sort, passed out by these strange and sad people. But they were taken seriously enough by the police who put a twenty-four-hour sentry on the twins' house. They call themselves Animal Right Supporters, all well and good: I'll say no more.

The other problem with the urban fox population is the likelihood of rabies getting into the country and becoming endemic in the urban foxes. Lots of them have Sarcoptic Mange now, which occasionally we see in the rural environment – the disease being carried by fox lovers releasing urban foxes into rural areas. Not being rural foxes, they cannot cope in the countryside where they wander about looking for Kentucky Fried Chicken detritus. They are quickly shot because they are not afraid of humans. Rabies would spread through them just as quickly and the consequences to the human population would be catastrophic.

If a fox can take and kill a six-week-old lamb, it can surely take and kill a baby. It will happen, because there are not too many young lambs in Fulham and foxes have to eat.

Leaning on the draining board staring, still half asleep, out of the kitchen window, I watch a dog fox come into the house yard through the carriage shed. He seems in no hurry, checking nonchalantly the tops of the dung heap wall for any kind of food left there, picking out what I think must be some flaked maize. He wanders over the dung heap, sniffing, turning over delicately with his paw some straw, to lick out an eggshell that lies beneath.

They are beautiful creatures, foxes, and thereby perhaps the cause of part of the problem. The greatest rift between town and country people is over the question of killing them. There are probably now more foxes in urban areas than in the country. The urban foxes show no fear of humans and that is where the danger lies. There are ever more attacks on humans by urban foxes.

This fox I am watching is a beautiful specimen, certainly not a last year's cub by the size of him. As I watch he leaves the muck heap and ambles down past the front of the stable block, into the next yard. On his left is a range of fifties-style open-fronted cattle sheds, on his right a large metal-stanchioned barn from perhaps two decades earlier. In this barn is stored barley straw, from two harvests ago. The fox walks down the yard to halfway, then stops, sits down and begins scratching his ear with one of his rear paws. All this looks sweetly innocent, a very handsome dog fox scratching his ear, sitting on his bottom. Now watch! Tobey*[12] stands, shakes himself, a final glance around, then with one leap he lands four square by the barn stanchion, to promptly disappear behind it into what must be a gap between the straw bales.

'Ho Tobey! We know where you live!'

He has chosen his living quarters in one way quite cleverly. Who would think of a fox living twenty feet below where the straw yard chickens – free-range birds – roost at night? It must be better than living in a damp musty earth[*13], a lot warmer and drier in the straw stack.

But (and here is the rub), if you pick up an adder it will bite you. If you stir up a hornets' nest with a stick, they will barrel out of that nest and sting you – and if you leave a fox near chickens, Tobey will kill them. That is the way of things. Now it is said that we could fence the chickens in. That would be costly and inconvenient; the fowls would hate it. They have been a self-perpetuating flock for about thirty years, pure-bred magnificent birds.

The other option is to shoot you, Tobey. I'll make a good job of it. You can't help doing what foxes do and you'll be dead before the sound of the rifle reaches you.

***

To ride out on an early June morning as the natural world is just waking or perhaps going to rest, as is in the case of foxes, badgers, and otters, is to see nature at its most relaxed. Animals have their routines the same as humans do, when they take up residence in the area and make it their own territory. They soon enough can be seen doing the same things in the same place daily, at roughly the same time.

The dawn chorus is thinner now, the main of the resident birds have done their nesting, raised their young and so their singing is no longer so long or vibrant. The immigrant birds of summer, the warblers, so many different species, are the birds that sing loudest now. The garden warblers and the wood warblers sing against each other, stating their territories, challenging each other to stay clear.

At this time, every year, the young tawny owls come unstuck in the dewy grass of the mornings, flying well and easily by now. They never seem to catch on that their soft downy feathers soak up the dew, making them heavy and rendering them suddenly flightless. The parents know where their young are so it's best not to interfere unless the soaked bird is really distressed. In this case, place the bird on a fence post or flat surface to dry out, in sight of where it was first found. Beware if taking it home to dry it out in the warm, unless you feel the need to have an owl living with you for the next decade or so.

In Hampshire and Devon, the first bird to wake and proclaim the dawn is the little wren; the cock bird song is loud and clear, belying the size of the singer. On a still morning it is audible from three hundred yards to the human ear. Earlier in the year the cock bird will have built several nests, a round ball of exquisitely woven grass, moss, hair, and wool (should they live in sheep country). The hen wren inspects them all, eventually choosing one to raise her brood of anywhere between six and a dozen chicks. The other nests remain, seemingly a waste of effort, but watch them quietly. As the nights get colder, they become roosts for that year's wrens, sometimes as many as a dozen full-grown birds in one nest. They are warm and snug and help the tiny birds survive.

Here, the blackbirds rise fairly early, second to the wrens, their song in June just as beautiful, but shorter now, perhaps less complex.

The windbreak that protects Lydgates and Tournament fields is made up of a pure stand of Japanese larch. The records tell us they were planted 102 years ago. There are two rows of three rows, with a rack*[14] between, wide enough to run a tractor or a pair of horses down.
The outside rows were never 'brashed'*[15] so their now huge branches sweep the earth, breaking the wind, creating the same

wonderful sound as a rigged sailing ship. As only the outside rows have branches, limbs and needles down to the earth, the wind slides through these, until it reaches the rack in the middle of the rows. Ride through here on a windy day, with some breast feathers from a pheasant in your pocket, drop them in a heavy blow then watch them fly upwards. The rack becomes almost a venturi tube, the wind being sucked out through the crowns of the trees. In the lee of these trees, sheep were folded on turnips. Even in the winter, the larches were enough to shift the wind.

Riding through the rack at this time of the year, and this time of the day, will show you how many birds are produced by these conifers. Great tits, blue tits, coal tits, yellow hammers and long-tailed tits, the great tits and blue tits generally occupy the dozens of bird boxes put up for them over the years. The trees run away towards the east for about 400 yards, curving gently this way and that so that the rack does not become a wind tunnel; also, I suspect so that my forebears could get close to the small herd of fallow deer that elect to live with us to augment ours and our friends' meagre meat rations, when the country goes to war.

Venison from the fallow deer is by far and away the best to eat, I think, dense but not coarse-grained like the red deer venison. We don't see many roe deer. There are plenty quite close in the New Forest but they don't seem to like us. It is, maybe, that our large tracts of arable put them off. All the tractor work that happens with them are a great disturbance, or maybe having to cross great wide open spaces to get from one copse to another makes them uncomfortable.

There are about forty to fifty fallow deer, spread fairly thinly from home, up through to Mottisfont and out towards Embley. We see them mainly through the winter. I think they come for the swedes and certainly eat enough of them. They never seem to eat a whole one, just wander along taking a bite out of one, then another. I can understand why our neighbours in Devon despair of the red deer damage to their swede crops.

***

'Up the hill at Lydgates,' is what we say indoors, but until we had a home in Devon, we didn't really know what hills were. From the driveway to the top of the rise in Lydgates cannot be more that sixty feet, taking 400 yards to get there. It was nothing more than a very controlled genteel passage on a toboggan. Reaching the top on this day, we came to the corner, where the windbreak of larches angles north and the corner is marked by a western red cedar. Why, I have no idea, but a beautiful tree now, some three feet and more across its butt. There is a field gate here: its supporting post is metal, ornate, something like the lamp posts along the Victoria Embankment.

It looks incongruous and lonely. Every year there are always two families of nuthatches that live in the red cedar tree. Their sharp drumming echoes down along the rack. They are quiet, beautiful little birds; only in the spring do they make themselves heard; their mainly single note call and drumming last only a few short weeks.

Riding now in the open, along what was the old hedge line between the two fields, Lydgates and Tournament, it is noticeable how different the bird life is. Out here we see skylarks, meadow pipits, wheatears and grey partridge or, more to my liking, English partridge or even just partridge: anything that sets them apart from the French or red-legged partridge. Gaudy creatures these, who sound more like miniature turkeys: they are slightly larger than the grey partridge, but do not fly with nearly the same panache. To hear the grey partridge calling on a summer evening as the countryside goes to rest, for me, is the sound of England.

Several nest at the base of the south-facing wall in the kitchen garden, under the fruit trees and bushes. They are safe here; the kitchen garden is fox-proof; raptors are just not tolerated lest they take the families of goldfinches that nest in the apple trees. So important are they that a small patch of teazles is grown in the wet corner where the land drain has broken. To see the goldfinches on the drying teazles in autumn is something that rarely happens anywhere now, a sight to remember to store in your memory.

***

It is often said that a farmer's boot is the best farm management tool. In other words, a farmer needs to walk his crops and wander through them regularly. A better tool perhaps is a farmer on a horse, riding around and through the crops. In these days of tramlines,*[16] a ridden horse can pass through the crop without causing damage. The perspective you get from the saddle looking down into the crop is much better – the leaves of the cereal are all visible, much easier to see and to catch any disease before it spreads and damages the crop.

There is a double fence between us and our neighbour, two rows of barbed-wire fencing, five strands high. The gap between the two fences is never less than ten feet. In places between the two fences, a drainage ditch runs, deep and usually full.

Close by, where the two buzzards were killed not long ago, there is a crossing place, with gates either side, so this has become 'the double gates on the March Fence'. The word 'March' has nothing to do with the time of the year, rather it comes from an old farm map where the division between us and our neighbour is marked with a double row of crosses. Between the crosses, in several places written in a beautiful copperplate hand are the words 'March Fence'. The land agent at the time originated from Monmouthshire in the Welsh Marches; he brought the name with him and it has remained so. The origin or the March Fence is not obscure in any way for the fence was constructed to keep our cattle away from next door's. The fence is a part of what today is called bio-security. Our cattle are cleaner than next door's animals and were a T.T. herd*[17] a lot earlier. The fence is to stop the cattle taking each other's breath or touching noses, when next door's cattle could perhaps pass on TB to our herd.

***

Field names, stream names, names of woods and copses are a fascinating subject; it is usually the social history to some degree of an area. I have written about Lydgates Field. Lydgates was a monk who lived in a hut in the far corner of the field at some time in the fourteenth century. Why he was there I do not know but live there he did for some thirteen years. He paid no rent and was supplied with his needs from the farm. I can only assume that my forebears had a more benevolent attitude to the clergy than is the case now.

Tournament Field was, as the name suggests, a field which was licensed to hold tournaments – knights with lances, swords, and other appendages. Whether they were necessarily chivalrous I do not know, but probably not. It was a rough era.

Flushing Field meadow goes back to sheep farming. Before the rams went into the flock, the ewes were 'flushed': that is, their food intake was increased and the quality enhanced. This was thought, correctly, to increase the amount of eggs a ewe produced, leading to more twin lambs. Flushing fields, you will note, always caught more of the sun than the other fields, for the sun and daylight again increased the fecundity of the ewes.
Having just looked up *flushing* in the very latest Oxford dictionary, I realise how far from our rural roots everything has moved. The dictionary speaks of flushing the loo, flush as in a hand of brag or poker, flush as in 'blush', nothing at all about its rural meaning.

Most Manor Farms in the country will have a field named The Butts or Butts Field. This was the field where archery was practised. By law you were compelled to practise from your early teens till you were infirm, too old to pull a bow. It was an early form of national service I suppose, which won Agincourt and Crécy and numerous other less well-known battles. Football was proscribed. You were not allowed to spend your spare time at this game because it led to fighting, drunkenness and lewdness. There's not much new under the sun.

***

Once through the double gates, the world changes again as we ride into Ridge Copse. Here under the canopy of leaves the air is still almost chill at this time of day. Where the sun does break through, it looks almost like searchlights upside down. Long broad fingers of yellow light, probing and searching the leaf litter on the woodland floor, turning the heads of the delicate shade-loving flowers towards it, demanding their worship, fealty and homage.

These woods are 'keepered woods', managed by a gamekeeper. At this time of the year they are quiet places, overflowing with wild flowers and song birds. This is part of the gamekeeper's work, for, by keeping the vermin in check, the small birds flourish and there is never the sound of that chattering butcher, the magpie. You might well think the bird has become extinct when riding through this woodland and also absent is the carrion crow.

The trees, mainly oak, are between 200 and 300 years old; the under storey is hazel still coppiced.*[18] There is enough timber on this estate to make it necessary to employ forestry workers, and it shows. The woods are well kept, with more than an eye to the wildlife. A strict rotation of cutting and thinning the softwood is maintained which may look just a higgledy-piggledy mix of trees but actually is a well-thought-out plan: to keep the estate in timber products, softwood and hardwood. Softwoods are generally conifer, non-deciduous trees bearing needles. Larch is a soft wood, a conifer that drops its needles in the autumn. Hardwoods come from the deciduous trees, broadleaf trees that lose their leaves every autumn: oaks, beech, sycamore, chestnut. There are exceptions: holly, for example, keeps its leaves in autumn but its wood is still classed as a hardwood.

The softwoods are mainly used in construction, boat building, fencing with the timber suitably treated. The hardwoods are for furniture and for more expensive construction work. Further into the wood is the hazel that was cut last year and is in the first stage of re-growth, their thin whippy shoots growing up to the light, about two feet high now. The hazel stools*[19] equidistant, planted in rows that only now show, are a home to small birds. The fissures, holes and cracks within the stumps house robins, hedge sparrows, pipits, warblers, and in this wood particularly, the nightingale.

The bluebells are still in profusion in this area of short coppice. The wood is a little late here as it slopes somewhat towards the north and it lays a little damp. What vision the forester must have had when he first laid out the wood. Cutting and digging the drainage ditches, planting the young oaks, in long lines, about thirty yards apart, when the oaks were established, pushing the hazel whips into the earth. They are warm woods, shelter for the thousands of pheasants, an undisturbed paradise for the brown hares which live the around the margins.

Though it is still early in the day, the 'straw ride'*[20] has perhaps two dozen pheasants feeding on it; away from them are grey partridges, feeding quietly in a group – there must be at least fifty, they ignore my passing, barely shifting away from my mare's feet. I don't think they recognise anybody mounted as human. The end of the ride is closed off with a locked five-bar gate; these farm gates are there to keep the cattle out of the woods and unwelcome humans. The gates stop people driving into the woods 'to have a picnic' or 'to pick flowers' or to poach pheasants. The gamekeeper soon gets to know the felons; people who just walk in the woods along the rides, appreciating the birds and flowers, are usually welcome, depending on the time of year.

Look back from where you have come; see the beauty of the woodland. The man who was in charge of planting it lies buried in the local churchyard, unknown and unremarked. His legacy so much more important than any other artist, this man's art changes with the seasons, a haven for both men and wild creatures. For some years, coming through this wood on my pony, I would see by this gate a 'keeper's gibbet'. A fascinating thing for a small boy, hung on a wire would be a line of decomposing bodies, of 'vermin' – squirrels, magpies, jays, crows, rats, stoats, weasels, sparrow hawks, kestrels, anything that predated on game birds, small birds or leverets. Foxes were not hung on the gibbet. They were skinned and the pelt cured for the London fashion houses, an income for the gamekeeper.

The gibbet was there to show the estate owner, land agent and head keeper that this particular keeper was doing his job properly. 'Properly' as in 1950s, there was not the rearing of game birds on the scale there is today, so any predation had to be stopped. It was always apparent that an estate that kept the predators in check produced more song birds. The moorland keepers, looking after red grouse, knew that by killing the vermin they produced more red grouse, and not only the game birds but also the upland wading birds, curlew, lapwing and other plovers. So a delicate balance was maintained, a balance not to be wrecked by raptors.

Today things are somewhat different; more pheasants and partridges are artificially reared for shooting. Whether or not it offends some people, the fact remains it is a very important part of the rural economy. As a very famous naturalist and gamekeeper once said to me, 'All the trapping and vermin control in the world doesn't make the numbers up for half a day's shooting. We just rear enough so that the predators don't make the difference,' but in another generation, there will be no songbirds in the woods and fields: the raptors, corvidae and domestic cats will see to that.

Writing this book to me is like wandering around in the country; I'm afraid I may have made it seem idyllic. Well, it is mainly – the views, the wildlife, real villages with real rural people living in them, watching the farming year. Agriculture is the authentic and beating heart of these islands of ours.

There are things that detract from it; I will write about them briefly, and then choose to forget them as far as possible. The interference we have to put up with from government and quangos, people who know nothing of how we live, how we make a living and how we spend our leisure time and yet direct how the countryside is run. I am not going to qualify what I state, but just give a few examples of what makes us cross, what makes us seem like the grumpy people.

I will start with DEFRA, staffed by people so incompetent and ignorant of the industry they are meant to help and administer. If it wasn't so serious it would be funny. I will just say TB and badgers.

Next in the firing line is the RSPB. which in rural areas is generally known as the 'bird police'. The RSPB has been watching the decline of the small bird population since the 1950s; birds that were once common and widespread have now become rare. The RSPB seems at a loss to explain this; despite its wealth and scientists, it is much easier to blame modern agriculture and gamekeepers, allowing itself more time to inveigle money out of gullible urban people.

DEFRA and the RSPB are a nuisance, because of their ignorance. The RSPCA however, having once been an organisation that deserved and had the respect of the majority, have now put into practice a more radical agenda, fervently anti-field sports, anti-farmer and anti-culling, even of the most destructive of pests, for example foxes, grey squirrels, feral cats and mink. At one time it had the odious Jackie Ballard heading it, the ex-MP from Taunton; she made hunting her main platform in an election and lost. I remember she wept when the count was over; she claimed, 'The hunting people have done this to me.'

It didn't amount to a row of beans in the end; when the hunting ban went through, nobody took that much notice of it. It wasn't that the rural people are not generally law abiding, certainly more law abiding than the urban set, it was just Tony Blair. How could anybody take him seriously? After all he is nothing but a know-nothing Townie.

Tony Banks MP was another protagonist; he was referred to locally as 'Ranter Banks', always ranting and raving in the Commons; the subtlety of calling him 'Ranter' was lost on the Labour lot. Ranter was one of John Peel's hounds in the song – 'Ranter, Ringwood, Bellman and True'.

Some years ago, with the discreet help of the *Sunday Telegraph*, I instituted a national grey squirrel cull. This was to save our native red squirrel, pretty well as much of a pest as the grey squirrel, but at least it is our pest, a home-grown variety. They have two saving graces over the grey: they are very pretty, much less of a rat's cousin, and, as far as I know, are not given to killing and eating fledglings. For about two years I was vilified by the media, until with patience, we eventually got a fair hearing, again thanks to the Sunday broadsheets.

I must admit I was getting pretty fed up with some of the telephone calls, so when a lady called Naomi telephoned, I was about to give her a verbal broadside, until she explained what she wanted. Naomi was from Market Harborough and was having trouble with grey squirrels, magpies and rabbits in her garden. Could I help her? Naomi was certainly not the usual run of suburban lady; at seventy, widowed, she had learned how to cope with the changes in society. In short, she was like a communal grandmother with an inner lining of pure steel. When I suggested she should get herself an airgun, instead of the usual shock, horror, at the suggestion, Naomi enquired where such things were available.

Four years on and Naomi has a state-of-the-art air-rifle, powerful, pre-charged*21 and silenced. Out four or five evenings a week now, the lady gets paid for keeping the local garden centres free of rabbits, squirrels and pigeons; not only that, she also supplies the local butcher with rabbits at two pounds a time. When the invitations come for lunch these days, which are very frequent, the invitation also carries a request, 'Can you bring your gun, please?'

I well remember the time when Naomi telephoned me at the outset of her new career: she had just got an agreement with the first garden centre. Her fee was ten pounds per week, the rabbits and pigeons hers to keep. That first week gave her the fee and sixteen pounds for neatly head-shot rabbits; since then she has gone from strength to strength, clearing feral pigeons from grain silos, and magpies and crows from a local pig farm. A modern-day hired gun, her clients applaud her ability and discretion and value her work; every town should have one.

Riding out through the park and onto the main road, we turn right and head up the hill on the White Parish Road. It is still too early for much traffic; the verges are wide here, a chance for a good scamper, a long pull uphill which will do me and my mare good. At the top of the hill, looking out right-handed in the distance are the chalk downs, now just an indistinct blue-grey haze. On my left, the direction in which I am heading, after one hundred yards everything changes abruptly. The verdant green and denseness of the sward beneath the mare's feet become paler, thinner. There is a lot of last year's leaf fall still showing on the surface, showing the world there are not enough earthworms here, to pull them down: short of earthworms, short of fertility.

Further on the oaks give way to silver birch and a few spindly sweet chestnut, then eventually to silver birch and laurel brakes. The gardens along Gardners Lane have ornamental heathers growing in the shapely beds cut out in the well-trimmed lawns.

Under the birch trees, amongst the leaf litter, fingers of dark green gorse show through, plants trying to recover the ground they have lost; if left for two years these gardens would revert back to what they were, furze scrub and heather. In the space of seven or eight miles, we have crossed three bands of soil: alluvial deposit, the beginnings of the chalk downs and now, on the edge of the New Forest, sands.

Sands are probably the most difficult of soils, as the soil particles are bigger; when I write 'soil particles' I mean the tiny individual pieces of broken-down rock that makes the soil. Look at your bare feet when you walk from the sea onto the dry sand, and you can see then how big these particles are. They don't hold water or goodness, everything washes through, every scrap of limestone is leached*[22] out; hence the only plants that can live there are those that do not demand high fertility.

Having said all of that, there are pockets of fertility in the New Forest heath, farms and homesteads that have gradually built up their fertility over centuries. This has been achieved through stock farming and the application of manure, farmyard dung. This is termed the fertility of the hoof. The area will never grow wheat in any sense, but barley, oats and rye will yield some average tonnages. The area will grow grass well and fairly early, and if there is not too much rain, it can be grazed early to produce cheap milk. If the weather is wet, then every cow has five mouths, the one she eats with, the four others are her feet, which sink into soft ground and bury mouthfuls of grass every time she takes a step.

At the end of the day, farmland will produce what the soil type, climate, topography will allow it to. You can, if you want to waste money, force it to do other things, but be aware that if you try that approach it will cost you both money and heartache.

We rural people know this, have known it for centuries, so I am forced to wonder why, even in war time, anybody would try to grow potatoes on virgin New Forest heath. But try they did. Twenty-five tons of Arran Pilot sown, seventeen tons harvested. Seventeen tons of scabby*[23] tubers, not fit to eat, scabby because the ground was heavily dressed with basic slag*[24] at the same time as the seed was sown.

It was viewed with some amusement, despite the waste in war time of seed, fertiliser, and fuel; as one wag said: 'You'd have done better to try and grow tatties on Bournemouth beach, but they sowed mines there instead and they didn't grow either.'

The New Forest these days has become more or less a playground. There is yachting on the coast, out of Lymington and Christchurch to name but two ports, equestrian sports, walking, fishing, in fact a fully-fledged holiday area. I read just last week that Brockenhurst has more one million pounds-plus houses than anywhere in the country. There are some farms still functioning as farms, but mainly they are horsey places now. In one way it is quite a good thing, people bringing their wealth into an area. They spread some about and, as with farmyard manure, things flourish.

CHAPTER SEVEN
(July)

Mid-summer, the second hay and silage cuts are in the barns. The kale and Swedes have taken well, and from them another harvest of wood pigeons has been taken. Because of the heat, the birds were collected at the gun's meal times and tray-stacked feathered in a chiller, which Vicki, the game dealer, had parked in the bottom yard.

The gun shop has now compiled a fairly long list of vetted guns for pigeon shooting, so the whole thing has worked rather well. The team of guns who come here are very happy with their arrangements, stirring up competition by boasting about the number of pigeons shot and the quality of the meals provided. Such news travels quickly through the rural community; the farmers through the valley are amazed that they are being paid for pigeon shooting.

Another pigeon dealer is bringing pigeons down from the Fens, selling them to Vicki; he had a lucrative contract with a famous London food shop, until one of their customers found some lead shot in a pigeon. What do they expect, one wonders? They referred to the birds as 'wild pigeons'. As opposed to tame ones, I suppose.

The French, it seems, understand game much more thoroughly than the British urban housewife; they know better how to cook it and would probably be disappointed if a dinner guest didn't get to chew on a Number Five Shot – it adds to the authenticity of the Paris 'country table'.

More on the subject of food, can there be anything better to eat this time of the year than first early*[25] potatoes?

The contractors are in at the moment taking up the crop, not so early this year because a prolonged period of very cold weather in February. It was the same for everybody, so no real harm was done, our main competition Jersey Royals were no earlier than us. It is always good when this happens, people can then choose and compare. We grow Maris Bard which yield better than Royals and to my mind eat better. Certainly, some locals thought so; ours were grown quite close to the town this year, one grass field away from the main road. Inevitably, there was a spate of stealing, someone was driving across the grass field and helping themselves. It was not somebody pinching a few for the family, these people were taking them by the pick-up truck load. Next door's gamekeepers were informed, a trap was set, which was sprung within two nights.

Bill telephoned early one morning to say a black, half-ton pick-up was on its side in the field, two of its nearside tyres shredded, having come into contact with some bits of old chain harrow laid in the bottom of the trench we had dug. This time it was towing a trailer. They had meant to steal more this trip. The trailer in fact had been stolen a couple of weeks before from a farmyard further up the valley. All in all a good result, but galling none the less, that these people were able to spend their nights out poaching or stealing, because they didn't work in the daytime.

When the police eventually arrived to deal with the stranded pick-up and trailer, we were deemed to be at fault for growing potatoes so near the road: 'One hundred and fifty yards, it was asking for trouble.' Further, they would look into the legality of us digging a trench in our own field, to trap the pick-up and maybe injure its occupants. We should have blocked the gateway and track with earth walls; so we did, we had the chalk pit deliver five loads of clunch*[26], one in the gateway and one each side and back and front of the stranded pick-up, up very close.

When the police went to enquire at the local 'trailer park' no one wanted to claim the pick-up; it was registered to a non-existent company in Spalding. No further forward, the police gave it up as a bad job, paid the farm two hundred pounds to load the pick-up onto a lorry. The clunch was spread in a line toward the roadside gate. There was a new track to go here anyway, a pick-your-own was going to be established.

On every tide now more salmon run into the river, as soon as the tide begins to make. The pools at Redbridge become like the car park at the cricket ground, crowded. About two feet off low water on a rising tide the fish begin to go upstream, some in a crazy rush, shooting through the bridge arch, charging across the shallows, into the deeper water by the reed islands. Others with no seeming effort glide under the bridge, leaving a wash like a liner crossing the shallows, gliding steadily up towards Sandy Island. Because of the poaching problem it is best probably not to linger too long, looking too interested; the same people who set out to steal the potatoes, will be around at night trying to net or jag*[27] the fish, selling them to some of the hotels in Southampton.

It is one of nature's spectacles to watch them swim upstream. They rest, here and there, poke about inquisitively. I wonder if they are not refreshing their memories. Once, I saw a salmon pass under the bridge at Redbridge of astonishing size, it was huge, swimming quickly as though frightened. I drove as fast as the lanes allowed me, stationed myself by the fish pass at Nursling, lying down, hiding behind the grass next to the concrete pass.

Fish passed through the rushing flume, but not the one I had seen earlier. I watched for an hour, saw something over forty fish, from six to thirty pounds, swim past in front of my face, but not the big one. I drove up to Sadlers Mill where a small knot of men and boys hung over the bridge, gazing into the flying water. I could see by their animation I was too late: 'Biggest cock fish I've ever seen in the river,' a retired water keeper told me. Apparently, the rush of the fish pass meant nothing to it, he didn't hurl himself at it; he just swam up it. I wonder what his fate was; he would not have been welcomed upstream in the trout waters.

We are so very lucky in these islands; our rivers, lakes, ponds, and streams abound with fish, as industrial pollution hopefully becomes a thing of the past, they should continue to flourish. They can all be rescued from their past. Even the Thames has fish in the lower reaches now, an incredible achievement by dedicated people. Salmon now come into the river. There have always been a few trout upstream from Teddington. One day someone will catch a grayling in the Thames; then we shall know the river is clean.

When you consider that practically everything that a salmon runs into wants to eat him, it is something of a wonder that salmon exist. From the moment the hen salmon deposits her eggs in the gravel of the reds*28, where the freshwater eel predates upon them till the time they return from the sea, they are preyed upon. When the eggs hatch, the tiny alevins are eaten by practically everything; only when they become fry*29, and are able to hide and are not quite so subject to the water's movement, do they have any chance of growing on. They are tiny, about half an inch long. Other fish eat them with alacrity.
So they grow, as is normal in any river, the bigger fish eat them. I don't think a brown trout would consider any difference between any fry; if they are eatable, they get eaten. After about a year, depending on the availability of the food in the river, they change colour, and become 'parr' and have 'parr marks' on their flanks – these are like finger marks, darker than the rest of their bodies.

At roughly two years, they become 'smolts' and begin their journey to the sea. They gather in great rafts of fish, shoals a dozen yards long and wide, drifting and swimming downstream; if anything startles one fish it startles them all, they panic, and the surface of the water is whipped to foam in seconds. It does give the watchers an idea of how many smolts are moving. Other smolts join these huge shoals; at this stage each individual fish is anything between two and six inches long, again depending on what food was available to it. As the smolts reach the estuary, the bass feed heavily on them, until they reach the open sea.

Thereafter it is anybody's guess, and a very good thing that is, else every trawler out of Spain would intercept them. The smolts rapidly turn into the salmon we know, feeding in the food-rich waters of the North Atlantic; tagged fish from the southern chalk streams of England have been recorded on the eastern seaboard of Canada, far into the Arctic Circle, across the coasts of Iceland and Greenland – great wanderers, growing rapidly into the beautiful fish we know.

From then on, we do not really know. Salmon have lots of whims. They remain in the Atlantic for anything up to six years, or so their scale readings tell us. Let me put it this way; a salmon might decide to return to their parent river after a year at sea. These fish are called grilse. They come up their parent river generally in July or August. The proportion of these that go back to the sea is generally more than the fish that have been in the sea for two or three years. I don't know, and I suspect nobody does, what proportion of salmon stay at sea for two years as opposed to those that stay at sea for three, four or five years. The difference in their weight could be time at sea, where in the sea and what the feeding was like. I'm glad there is so much mystery surrounding their movements. They can never be wholly tracked down that way. If we knew everything about their movements, some people are so unscrupulous, they would be hunted to extinction in no time.

What whim turns them back towards their parent river I have no idea – probably the need to spawn – but turn they do and navigate back home. It is said they remember the taste and smell of their home river. The whole thing is one of 'Nature's Miracles'.

Our salmon must turn up Southampton Water from the Solent. If they are coming in from the south-west, does the water from the River Frome taste so different from the River Test? Certainly, the Frome doesn't have the estuary pollution that the Test does; coupled with this some of the fish come from the Itchen. That has something of a shared estuary with the Test. Something draws them strongly to their home river, where they hatched. They spawn in the headwaters, weakened and exhausted. They do not feed in fresh water. Most of them die, which does seem profligate. We see them in December and January, poor thin creatures, covered in fungus, turning end over end in the current, dead. Some hang up on the inner curve of the bends, rotting in the quieter spots of the river and you are forced to wonder whether the river will ever smell right again.

There are some fish that survive the rigours of spawning. These come drifting back down with the current, so thin and poor, you wonder how they survived the various fish passes without being smashed to pieces. These fish are known as 'kelts'; they rest in the shallows, their thin bellies on the gravel, their back sometimes out of the water. They are little more than a backbone covered with some flesh; when they reach the brackish water, that between salt and freshwater, they begin to feed. They stay in the river until they put on some weight, and at this stage they are known as 'mended kelts'. If you happen to hook one, during early spring fishing, it is your bounden duty to treat the fish as gently as possible, return it to the water as quickly as possible, hold it in your net or by the 'hand'*30, facing the flow of water until it has completely recovered from the stress of capture.

I am ambivalent at best about farmed salmon. I have seen it and the fish look wonderfully healthy, but I cannot help thinking it is like putting a swallow in a cage.

July, the air is filled with the scent of ripening winter barley; we are still growing the variety Sonja. It suits our soil and yields as well as any of the newer varieties. The combine harvesters have been outside in the sun. Their engines serviced and run up, every belt checked, renewed where needed and adjusted. Every grease nipple shows a splodge of pale-yellow grease, as do those on the balers, everything ready for the off.

The last of the spring wheat has gone to the flourmill, for a price that must have made Lord Rank's toes curl. The now empty grain store and cleaner are being vacuumed and disinfected. We use a contractor to do this, with all the correct safety gear. There is no sense in taking any sort of chance with anybody's health. The dust and spores from the grain are lethal to lungs; now that the dryer has been made fully automatic, there doesn't seem to be any reason to enter the building while it is running. The operator now controls the beast remotely, in a separate cabin with air conditioning.

The Shipping Forecast was at some variance to the forecast after the television news; the measured tones of 'Thames, Dover, Wight...' from the wireless are so much more believable than the arm-waving loon on the television. The television chap had promised a clear warm night. The Shipping Forecast chap threatened heavy drizzle with a light north-easterly wind – Force one or two, visibility poor.

It was daylight at four-thirty the following morning, not that the light helped – from the bedroom window the yard was not visible. Heavy drizzle and thick mist silenced the world. The earth, so warm after some hot sunshine for the past fortnight, now smoked with vapour, white and clinging. No matter, the potatoes are in their barn, clean of blight, their wonderful earth smell drifting through the ventilators, a cold draught being blown through them from the fans below, not enough to alter the skins, just enough to stop any mould. With luck they would be loaded out the next day, after the merchant had looked at them, to satisfy himself the potatoes were up to contract specification. We had eaten them with dinner that last evening. They were beautiful potatoes, surely there can be no better eating than the new season's lamb, coupled with Maris Bard potatoes and Hurst Green Shaft garden peas with freshly made mint sauce.

It was with some concern that I went to look at the barley, almost ready and looking like a heavy crop. Stormy weather, wind and heavy rain would flatten it. Heavy drizzle would flatten it more surely. You know if you walk in a storm in something like a tweed jacket, the cloth seems to shrug it off; walk in heavy drizzle in the same jacket and within ten minutes it has come through the cloth, your shirt is wet and the rain seeps through your trouser waist band – you are thoroughly soaked.
It is the same with barley, the drizzle will seem to wet it more thoroughly; it gradually goes down right across a field, never to rise again, making combining it more difficult and slower. On this occasion there was no need to worry, the barley was leaning but the ears, where the grain is, had not 'necked'*[31] any. They were still fairly upright.

There is an old maxim that states: When you think your barley is ready to harvest, go away on a fortnight's holiday.

Perhaps through impatience and the need to get the crop in before the weather breaks up, as the month moves on, it is difficult not to go every day and rub out a few ears between your palms. The grain feels ready in places, leave it a little, have patience.

News filters across the south of England that the 'combines are out' around Chichester, which makes everyone more touchy than ever. The combines are started every day; the farm mechanic tweeks any adjustments he imagines need doing, his reputation for the next year depends on a smooth harvest. There is no need to worry. The mechanic is German and has more than his share of Teutonic thoroughness.

On the nineteenth day of the month, the same as ever, the combines go out to cut the first barley fields. Unasked and unbidden, everyone leaves what they are doing elsewhere on the farm to come and watch; even the two farm secretaries arrive in a Mini, both in the shortest miniskirts, ever seen, scraps of coloured cotton, which raises the morale of the men.

Pretty soon the man on the combine will be a thing of the past; modern combines are controlled on a GPS. However, it is going to take a very brave man who first lets his combine 'out on its own'. If a jumbo jet can traverse the Atlantic, automatically, then it's a sure bet that a combine will cut cereal automatically shortly. The pilot of the jet is not much more than a sop to the passengers' sensibilities, anyway.

These days you can have your combine on tracks, huge rubber tracks that run the length of the machine; it gives great peace of mind on the alluvial soils on part of the farm. The alluvial soil, the silt left by the river, seems bottomless, fertile and friable when right, growing superb crops. There is one rule you don't forget though: if the combine starts to spin her driving wheels, when it had wheels, lift the bed and reel and get out. These days the combines skip over the soft ground, even after rain as long as the grain-hauling trailers are on hard ground nothing has to stop.

The moment arrives that we have been waiting for since last October. The combines move into the crop; as the yield falls onto the elevator the barley goes up into the drum, the engine's governors open a little, and dark smoke belches from the bellowing exhaust.

We are harvesting; the combines leave the outside round, close to the hedge – it is damper here and there some weeds, ox-eyed daisies and mayweed. This will be cut later and put in a separate trailer, either for cleaning or for the farm's own use.

The air now smells of freshly thrashed straw, it tumbles out of the rear of the combine, crushed and crimpled. The mechanic walks beside the machine listening to the individual sections doing their work. The new v-belts fitted over the winter smell of hot rubber as they bed themselves in; soon there is a sixty-foot row of stubble running up the field.
Perhaps I should explain how a combine works; even now I am in absolute awe of them. What it does is cut, thrash and separate the grain from the ear of the cereal, which it keeps in a collection tank on the machine. The straw is passed out over the straw walkers at the machine's rear.

The front of the machine is 'the head'; this has the cutting deck, much like a large finger-and-plate mower. Above this is the 'reel', which pushes the crop back into the combine. Crossways there is a large Archimedes screw, which pushes the crop towards the centre of the bed, to be picked up by a straw elevator, which feeds it into the drum and concave. This part of the machine does the thrashing or threshing depending on what part of the country you come from. The drum and concave have to be set precisely. The drum, which is like a large mangle wheel, has bars on it, which spin just clear of the concave. The straw passes through the gap between them. The bars knock the grains from the ears, without knocking them about too much. The grain falls through the machine into a tank with an auger in, which lifts it to the main tank from which it is augered out into the grain trailers.

The straw, now crimped up by its passage through the drum and concave, drops onto the straw walkers; by their reciprocating action, the straw is carried through the back of the machine and dropped in rows. The machine can have a spreader on the back, which spreads the straw thinly on the ground, if it is not required for baling.

The setting of the drum and concave is absolutely critical; the gap between the two depends on what is being thrashed and what the crop is. Loosely, whilst combining field beans the concave is going to have a wider setting than when ryegrass is being thrashed.
The first combines were called 'baggers' because they augered the seeds into bags. Two men rode on a platform on the side of the combine; when the bags were up to weight two and a quarter hundredweights*[32] in the case of wheat, they were tied and dropped onto the ground. Onto the ground! Fer Christsake! A slide onto a wagon would have made it easier I think, but that would be blasphemy.

The sequence of cutting cereals depends largely on where your cereals are grown, how high and how cold your area is, how early you can generally sow – a lot of it is in the lap of the gods.

In Hampshire, in theory, it runs winter barley, peas, spring barley overlapping into winter wheat and finally spring wheat. The prefixes of seasons are when it is sown. Winter wheat and winter barley are sown through the autumn. I have known years when we were drilling winter wheat in December, far too late, but you cannot best the weather. The spring sowing usually started in mid to late February, if the soil was warm enough. Spring wheat first, only because we had learned to be rather specialist at it, and it paid better than barley.

In fact we never 'drilled' spring wheat, rather we 'spun' it on through the fertiliser distributor onto prepared ground. This was for speed really, the more spring wheat we got in early the better; once April was with us, we would drill any ground left unsown with feeding barley.

Feeding barley, what does that mean? A feed barley is grown for tonnage; the bushel weight – that is weight by volume – has to be up to contract specifications, the moisture content the same, around fifteen or sixteen per cent and clean. That is, no more than a trace of weed seed in it. Another specification for barley is for malting, making beer.
We rarely achieved this because our crop rotation made the land a 'bit strong', that is, too fertile. Malting barley has to have a low nitrogen content in the kernel and when cut across the grain, should show the grains to have a flour in them. It was easier to achieve with certain varieties; it was not really of much interest to us, so we never grew it.

Wheat has two distinct uses, feed for animals and wheat for making bread with. Feed wheat varieties yield more per acre generally; it is softer, having a lower bushel weight. If milled it could make bread, but not the sort of bread we like to eat – it does not have enough protein or 'stretchability'*[33]; it lacks gluten.

Feed wheat varieties seem to break down quicker to the various fungal diseases that affect wheat, but maybe that is just my observation at home. Some of them have difficulty in making contract specification on bushel weight.

Milling wheat, or bread-making wheat as it is now generally referred to, can yield less than the feed wheats, but farmed properly the difference is not enough to make it uneconomic to grow. The price per ton paid is usually enough to cover the difference.

The grain is generally heavier by volume and even if it doesn't come up to milling specification on protein and hagburg*34 it will still command a premium over ordinary feed, if it is sold right, for export.

The farm needed barley for its own use, stock feeding, and also, a 'cereal exchange' with the merchant – that is, swapping loads of cereal for loads of cattle cake with a payment by us for the difference. The merchant lorries would arrive with the dairy cake, blow this into the feed bins, then load with barley to take back to the compound mill; transport costs were halved and the farm's cash flow was eased. We never grew much feed barley, about four hundred acres which was enough for our needs, with some over for selling to small pig producers.

We rather liked the challenge of growing the quality of the milling wheats; we were so close to the flour mill and the export terminal that we could deliver it ourselves and again save some of the cost of contracting hauliers.

Winter oats deserve a special mention. They were good as a crop to give land a rest from wheat, if the rotation got out of kilter because of the weather. We grew grazing rye for the dairy cows' 'early bite'*35, but we were just as likely to graze the winter oats as early bite, should the dairy animals require it. If the oats were grazed, the field would be shut up for a few weeks to see if the oats recovered sufficiently to think about letting them go on to harvest. This would depend on the weather; a warm wet time would help them recover to grow on, but obviously they would not yield such a large crop. Against this though, the quality would always be there. Oats are a very amenable crop. The best of the grain would go as 'racehorse oats', the rest would go for human consumption; it's true the horses had the very best.

There is great play made on growing crops for fuel, as though this was something entirely novel. For centuries we grew the fuel for the motive power of this farm, hay, oats, linseed, straw for their bedding. The workhorses were fuelled by the best of everything. Even when steam arrived in the form of tractors, stationary engines etc. mostly they were fuelled on wood, felled on the place.

Very soon there is a large tract of barley cut, enough so that there is space for the balers to begin their work. The combines have cut around the fields' outside, now they are cutting up and down, with room to turn on the headlands. Shortly the field is dotted with today's huge round wrapped bales; they are a very efficient way of gathering up the straw, but no use at all for the smaller farmer, because of the equipment needed to shift them about. There are lots of smaller farmers in this part of Hampshire that rely on us for a supply of normal-sized square bales, and to that end what looks today like a miniature tractor is baling along the centre rows of the thrashed straw.

It already looks quaint and old fashioned, but this is how it was done only five or six years ago. The bale sledge catches the bales and dumps them in batches of twenty. There had been a chronic shortage of straw because of the last year's wet weather, and so, like locusts, the horsey people and the smaller farmers descended on the field. It was all a little like a Giles cartoon. There was a lady with a Morris 1000, wanting one bale for her rabbits, another with a Land Rover and stock trailer and various small tractors and trailers, all following the small tractor and baler. They had been instructed to go to the farm office, pay for what they wanted, come to where the combines were and take what they had paid for. Nobody checked what they had, there wasn't anybody with the time to do it, or the inclination.

The computers on the combines were giving a blow-by-blow account of how much had been cut and what the yield was thus far. It was always a puzzle to know why one part of the field yielded barley a ton to the acre and other parts over three. It was something to do with the soil's structure, because it tested the same all over, structure or trace elements. Where basic slag had been applied, the crops looked healthier when growing and green, but they didn't yield any differently than where ground chalk had been the dressing.

Back in the latter part of last February, when this barley we are cutting was no more than a couple of inches high, there were four or five hares playing about on the field. They had boxed, run around in circles, and eventually, after mating, settled down to normal life. As the barley grew the hares still criss-crossed the area, leaving runs over the fields; as it grew taller, they still used the same runs, but these closed in over the top of the hares. Now that the fields are almost laid bare of cover, the runs show as tiny track-ways, tiny grey/brown pathways, worn down to the bare earth. We have not seen any hares today, because we had the dogs into the crop first thing, to drive them to safety into the copse.

An occasional pheasant bursts from just in front of the knife and reel. Stupid creatures, pheasants. This one nearly lost his legs. There had been some quail calling from this area earlier in the week; I say 'from this area' because quail seem to have the ability to throw their voices. You hear them in one place, but when you go there with dogs in the hope of surrounding a couple with vine leaves in the Aga, they are not where they sounded as though they were.

The best way to put them in your game bag is to go after them with an English Pointer. Some years there are hundreds of them, others barely any at all. They are summer visitors; when they do come there are hundreds of them. It is said that quail were the manna that the Israelites lived on when they were wandering in the desert.

The rule was, have enough for just the day, otherwise they would not keep – which is quite right, without the refrigerator they would be off in a day. They are good to eat, pluck them clean, gut them out, then place parsley and mint fresh chopped into the cavity, twenty minutes in the Aga's top oven, no more, else they will go dry.
There will not be many rabbits showing today. The Myxomatosis was just a month ago, this time so badly that the air stank of death for two weeks or more. I can remember the arable land back in the early fifties: despite all the ferreting and shooting, every field had a rabbit-grazed headland on every side, going into the crop for many yards. The other thing I can remember well is seeing for the first time a rabbit in the later stages of the disease – the huge swollen pus-filled eyes, the stink of his rotten flesh and agony of the poor creature. I wept for the shame of it, then anger came, then hatred for the men who had invented and spread the disease. Rabbits were a destructive pest for sure. They ate the food we grew without the care of ration books, but in truth we didn't do without. I was eleven years old, food was severely rationed, but I don't remember ever being hungry. The ration book never seared my soul, Myxomatosis did.

Now, as then, rabbits are becoming a pest again, nothing like they were before Myxie. Few people of my age, least of all me, eat rabbit pie these days. The smell of them cooking conjures up the day I saw a rabbit dying, dying of a despicable disease conjured up in a laboratory.

Obviously, I have shot and ferreted out hundreds of rabbits before and since those days, but it was done fairly. They were always given law. Now when I see a rabbit on the far side of the back lawn, I can only smile. So what if it eats on a few flowers, has a good chew on the shrubs, that is what rabbits do.

It has taken four days to cut the winter barley, only because of the very heavy dews, which stopped us getting on early, and prevented us going on into the night. There was plenty of time in theory, the days had been very hot, but the valley was always damp and misty early on. The hire combine has been delivered to the farm, slightly smaller than our own. The peas are really too early this year and have caught us on the hop.

The merchants who are buying the crop are sending a man down from Wisbech to make the decision about cutting them. When we start, there will be no stopping, only heavy rain will delay us. When he arrives he is immediately christened 'Postie' because his accent sounds very like the 'Singing Postman', who came from Fakenham way. He took it in good part; having looked at the peas, he agreed that the next day would be a good day to start and discussed the question of drying the peas, which in truth was a matter of blowing cold air through them.

They had to arrive in Wisbech, green but with no mould, so the sooner they had the outside dampness taken from them, the sooner they could leave the farm. They were destined for Japan, semi-cooked in a sweet batter-looking coating, in half-kilo packets. Rather them than us; sounded very fiddly, half-kilo bags.

The combines waddled away to the pea field ready to be cleaned out, meanwhile the bales of straw were going in different directions, some away from the farm, others to be stacked where we needed them. The cattle yards needed the big round bales. The calf pens and pigs used the small bales. By the end of the day they should be cleared. Later that evening, trying to get on the track of a particularly troublesome fox, I found myself on the edge of the stubble, amongst the last of the small bales left on the field. Standing in the shadow of a stack of bales, I listened to the evening. Behind me, a blackbird was pink, pink, pinking and the first of the evenings tawny owls began 'tuning up'. Tuning up does seem to cover what they do, almost a throat-clearing exercise, followed by rasping hiccoughs before the proper hoot comes. Then there is the whistle of pinions as a line of ducks circle overhead, before falling line astern onto the stubble. The ducks' (females) calling is quiet continuous soft quacking, which means there is food here.

It was a wonderful evening for just watching the ducks flying overhead, down toward the estuary; hearing the feeding notes they turned in a large circle and came arrowing in, in a rush of wind passing over stiff wing feathers. They were no more than twenty feet away and had no idea I was there. They fed greedily on the thrashed weed seed and what barley grains had 'come over the back'*[36] of the combines.

There are sounds in the country that gladden the heart, give you enormous pleasure in their remembering. The call of geese is one such noise. They sweep in low across the stubble, about six feet off the ground, turn in a circle making height as they do, before opening their huge wings to land deftly onto the cut barley field – magnificent. They call and gaggle for a few seconds, bobbing their beautiful heads up and down, looking for their mate. They soon settle to eating grain, right across the track that I know Tobey the fox is going to take. Rather than have this happening, keeping the stacked bales between myself and the geese, I get back to the run in the hedge I think he will come through and have a long and satisfying pee on it, then go back to the bales and watch.

The geese began to get uneasy, lifting their heads more; the fox was on the move probably. Without warning there he was, walking nonchalantly along the headland, pretending to ignore the wildfowl on the stubble. The ducks and geese followed his progress, ready to spring into the air should the fox get any closer. He sat and began scratching his ear with his hind foot.

This was just a distraction; looking at him through the 'scope' on my rifle, I recognised him as the one from the straw yard.

Suddenly, the fox began to behave oddly, turning round and round at speed, chasing his tail. The wildfowl were transfixed, watching his every move. The fox rolled over and over, then went back to tail chasing; he was now very close to the geese. There was a loud clapping of wings when I walked from my hiding place. The ducks fled and looked like heading for the river, the geese rose flew fifty yards then landed again. They were Canadian Geese, so half tame. I could see that the fox was in two minds about running away, so I flung a flint at him.

This only made him trot away to some bales lying out; he settled down by the side of this, with only his ears showing. This is what happens when foxes become unafraid. Tobey was now a potentially dangerous animal. There is something about the noise of metal on metal that wild animals recognise as a danger signal. All too late for this animal, the bullet was through his brain before he heard the bang; if you give insolent foxes any quarter you are begging for trouble. I have no doubt that this one was emboldened by the sudden lack of rabbits, guilty of killing a couple of tame rabbits on a lawn in the village, then, rather ironically really, he slew nine of Mrs Pegram's hens in her garden in daylight.

Mrs Pegram was a leading light in the League Against Cruel Sports, so there is a lady who was not going to get too much sympathy. She was in fact a strange, complex woman, a forensic scientist who behaved like a fish wife in the presence of anybody involved in field sports and was entirely irrational about foxes. As far as Mrs Pegram was concerned I was wholly to blame; foxes in her experience did not kill chickens, tame rabbits or lambs. She claimed I had captured the fox, starved it, then somehow let it go in her chicken run, where, being hungry, it had killed her hens. Further to this she was demanding compensation because the starving fox had obviously come from our farm, and the dead hens scattered about the garden had traumatised her children.

It was far too beautiful an evening to trouble oneself about a mentally deranged female. The sky away to the west was deep red, with thin striations of dark blue lines of high cloud. It needed photographing really; if an artist tried to paint it, it would look garish and unreal. Two huge skeins of geese flew from the east into this sunset, which made it more unreal somehow, like a porcelain plate painted by a fanciful artist.

These past few days have been fiercely hot, the evenings contrastingly cool, seeming chilly by comparison. The dark earth beneath my feet pulsed warm through my shoes. The stubble crisp and smelling like biscuits, only when moving over it and the short barley stems popped and crackled, would you be aware that rain was on the way.

Troubles never come in ones, that is why they are called 'troubles'. The representative from the merchants who were buying the peas, arrived with the news that his company was 'going into receivership'. They would not be able to take the peas; a fax would arrive to confirm this. He sounded desperate, his job was likely gone along with his house and home.

This left us with some choices to make. One, the peas could be ensiled – that is make silage with them and feed them to the dairy cows. Two, let them mature further into dried peas and feed them to the dairy cows in a mix with barley, chopped straw and molasses. Three, contact the Japanese firm, end users of the peas, and sell them direct.
The second option was taken. There was a fairly big subsidy for growing protein crops, even if they stayed on farm. Also, we would never lose control of them. Coupled with the now homeless peas, there was a strongly worded lettered letter from Mrs

Pegram's solicitor, telling me she was 'going for compensation' because it was obvious the fox that had killed her chickens belonged to me, and as such I was responsible. There was also the question of her children being traumatised to be dealt with.

By lunchtime, an agreement had been reached with the merchant who we did the bulk of our buying and selling to. The peas would be utilised by them on a load for load basis, dairy cake for peas, a straight swop; the contractors would arrive forthwith.

The fox shot the evening before was put in the back of the Land Rover and driven to Middlebridge Street, the home of Mrs Pegram. As she was not at home, I hung the dead fox on her fence with some baler twine, then dropped a letter, which one of the farm's secretary's had typed, through her post box. The letter was extraordinarily well mannered and solicitous, asking if she would be so good as to identify the fox as being the one that had killed her chickens. I realised that it would be tricky for her, because the bullet had entered the fox's left eye and exited from the throat. If she wanted me to dispose of the fox, to telephone and I would return for it. I heard nothing more of the matter.

With nothing now ready to cut, the combines were brought back to their barn; it was quite a good thing in fact because it allowed us time to start clearing the dung from the barns that had housed the dairy cows over the winter. When the dairy cows were brought in under cover, they slept on deep straw. This was not cleaned out every day like stables; rather, more straw was added, a clean top layer. This gradually built up over the winter, barley straw soaked in urine and cow dung; by the end of the winter the muck was probably four feet deep, trodden down by the cows' feet. It drained and dried when the cows went out in the spring and eventually reached a stage of perfection, a very valuable heap of dark, rich, semi-composted plant food.

Now that there was some cereal stubble, the slurry lagoon

could be emptied at the same time. Slurry is pure cow manure, cleared daily from the concrete areas where the cows feed on delivered food, silage, hay, sugar beet pulp and kale, if the land is too wet for the animals to go out to graze it. You can only imagine what a mess six hundred cloven hooves make on wet ground. Beyond this the animals' feet get soft and subject to damage and a disease known as 'foul of the foot', which is endemic throughout southern Hampshire in the soil. Nothing knocks their milk yield quicker, I think.

Footbaths help. In the summer we walk the Shorthorns through the river, which beautifully cleans their feet between the claws*[37]. The Ayrshires who live further towards the town are lighter animals, more skittish. They are too highly strung for paddling games. Ayrshires hate disruption in their lives. You may put a Shorthorn in a foot-trimming crush with a bowl of cake in front of her; she will moan about having a manicure but allow you to do it.

Getting any of the Ayrshires in the crush is the first problem. They hate it. They have lots of attributes: they produce milk on forage, the hay, silage etc. better than the Shorthorns do, despite their slight frame and small capacity to pack away food. They do not have the foot problems of the heavier breeds, which is a blessing. Trimming an Ayrshire's foot with a hoof cutter is nobody's idea of fun. It doesn't happen now because most calves are de-horned with an electric iron early in their lives, but when Ayrshires had horns, they were downright dangerous. But they are very pretty animals, with very fine skins, generally wonderful conformation, and great liquid brown eyes. I must own up to the fact that, at an agricultural show, the first thing I go and look at is the Ayrshires in the cattle lines.

Within the week both dairy barns have been dug out, and the resultant molten muck spread on the barley stubbles and a grass field being ploughed shortly to be sown with winter wheat. The air is perfumed with the smell of spread dung, I can imagine that people not used to this find it fairly offensive, but that is what we do and have done for centuries; get used to it.

When somebody asks you in the pub, 'How many days grouse shooting have you booked?' you suddenly realise that two-thirds of the year has gone. They are talking about 'driven grouse', where the birds are driven over the butts*[38] by armies of beaters. This is now far too an expensive pastime for me and for most folk I know. Going to the highest bidder, it is taken up by City people, Americans and Arabs. Grouse shooting for me has never been more than a couple of days at most, walking behind far-ranging English Pointers. Shooting at most a dozen brace in a day of hard walking, for somebody who hates walking through and over slip-slides of heather two days is enough. Given the choice of days, shooting driven grouse in Scotland or driven partridge at Six Mile Bottom, Sutton Scotney or Micheldever, I would opt for the partridge, but this is just me!

The weather has remained very hot and dry, the milling wheat is well forward, the berries well formed and dark brown. A telephone call from the flourmill reflects last year's wet harvest: 'will we have any wheat fit to mill by the twenty-first or -second of the month?' He will be willing to pay 'old-crop'*[39] price for it. Would it be possible to come out and have a look?
An offer not to be refused; selling grain is like a duel, you want as much as the merchant or mill will pay. They want to pay as little as they can. The flourmill had rather shown their hand. Telephoning for grain showed they were fairly desperate, but the manager was a very canny Scot; best to tread very carefully. Our output of wheat would only make about a week's milling. The mill was the largest in Europe; at most we would only have two hundred tons ready by the due date, so what was the game?

When the mill manager arrived, he announced he wasn't going to pay the same price as he had given for our July-delivered spring wheat. Well, this new crop was not of the same quality, we knew this, but we were putting ourselves out. So it went on for about half an hour; in truth he had not yet seen the wheat. Above the wheat that they went to inspect there was a heat haze, the earth radiated heat, and such a situation was not good for wheat just coming to ripeness. From ripeness to shrivelled is only a few days, when all the important wheat protein migrates to the skin and the germ dies. It would want constant monitoring. A deal was done in the field with no recourse to the laboratory; the wheat was good; at a pinch it would be right by the week's end. We had never cut wheat so early with a combine harvester.

In the days of the binder[*40] it would be just right. The first binders cut the crop, gathered it into stooks like a bunch of flowers; it was then tied around with a few straws of the same wheat and stooked, that is put up in groups to dry.

Later the binder had a knotter, which made life easier. The sheaves could be handled better and, when put into stooks, they stayed upright. The artists' conception of harvest was well adrift from reality. There were no weed-killers in those days and the sheaves would have had lots of thistles in them, which transferred their spikes into the bare flesh.
Thatching companies require wheat straw for their work; it has to be cut with a binder and stooked[*41], and it can then be left to mature a little. The sheaves are carted into the farmyard and stacked, ready for the thrashing box[*42] to come and thrash the grain out. Because of its design, the thrashing box does not break the backs of the straw stalks. They are re-tied and stacked in the dry, ready for somebody's new roof. One of the farm secretaries telephoned the flourmill to let them know we were about to start the milling wheat. Three very smart German cars pulled onto the stubble after the first rounds were cut. Samples were taken which were rushed away to the mill.

Within half an hour one of the girls arrived smiling. The wheat was up to our verbal specification, giving the nod to the other two combine drivers to start cutting. With the ground so hard it was possible to have the merchant's big artic lorries on the field, which were soon being filled straight from the combines. By evening, that part of the field, which was right for the flourmill, had been cut, and silence descended again as everyone made their way back to their homes, offices, or the pub.

Indoors, rather weary, there were four telephone calls complaining about the noise and dust from the harvesting going on, one about lights from the combines sweeping across their windows and a very irate new citizen to the town complaining about a fox that had slain his daughter's pet rabbit, demanding compensation.

In the past it was called 'doing a cousin Jack on him'. These days, after the film, it was expressed as 'doing a Crocodile Dundee on him' – basically filling the 'townie' up with lies and nonsense, bamboozle him with 'Tha's a scientific fact, see', and see how much money you were able to extract from him at the same time. Southern gamekeepers and Scottish ghillies are past masters at this sort of thing, and the head keeper from next door was one of the best. He convinced the complaining chap whose child's rabbit had been killed, that he would sit up and wait for the fox at night; 'And I promise you, Sir, we shall have him.' He also persuaded him that the fox had come from the east side of the river, because with it being so hot and sunny in the daytime, the tarmac roads wafted their smell of hot tar upwards, which is very injurious to the fox's sense of smell, laying himself open to danger so they would not in fact cross tarmac roads in such hot weather. He almost had me convinced with that one!

As harvest progressed all over the county, more and more foxes lost their sanctuary in the cereal crops, making new homes in the woods and hedges. That year's cubs became especially vulnerable as they wandered about looking for their own territory. It was therefore easy for the keeper to produce a freshly shot fox after 'lying up' in the wood opposite the gardens; in fact, he had not been near that wood. The townie was happy when he saw the dead fox, bloodied and broken, and, no, he didn't want it as proof. He gave the keeper thirty pounds, happy that the pet rabbit had had justice.

It had taken fourteen days and for me eight nights in the dryer, not as bad as it sounds, losing eight nights sleep in a fortnight. There was relief and satisfaction when the last trailer load of grain had been over the dryer. The silence closed in as at last I switched off. Drinks all round should have been the order of the day, but it was four in the morning and my only companion was one of the farm cats. Harvest was over. The grain was in the grain store and I needed a bath. Not the normal sort of bath, I needed the water of the river to wash the ingrained dust from my tired frame.
The sunset the previous evening had been spectacular. The dust in the air had produced great streaks of red. There had not been such a day's harvest for years. There had not been such tonnages of grain cut. In the north of the country the harvest was still going on. After the shortages that anybody over the age of twenty-five remembered vividly, this harvest should see that ghost laid to rest.

On the middle front seat of the Land Rover there was a change of clothes, towel and soap; it was almost a religious rite now, to bathe in the river when harvest was done with. It was not in any way properly light; looking down into the hatch pool the water looked dark and forbidding. The chill of the rushing water took the breath away until your mind and body adjusted to it. Bobbing about in the eddy of the fish pass, the soap lifted the dirt away; it was frowned upon indoors having soap in the river, but once a year couldn't hurt. It was really too cold, this rushing, sweet-tasting water. Later when the sun was up it would seem tepid almost but getting out left me shuddering with the chill of it.

The tide would now be coming in down at the estuary. The creeks and muddy runnels would be filling with the mud-thickened gloopy water, pushing into the reed beds. Tiny fish follow the advancing water, darting about, picking up even more tiny food particles. The soapy-looking bubbles that float up on the tide are dust covered; it has been dry and hot for seemingly weeks, and every movement creates more dust. When the rain eventually comes the whole world will smell earthy and warm; even the hot tarmac of the roads will exude a dusty hot smell before the life-giving water quenches its heat.

The dawn and tide race to fill the lower valley with light and water. The wildfowl and waders begin to rise and fly north, their right wings and sides the colour of amber in the pale sun, their left still in shadow. They are going up onto the stubbles to rest probably, having spent the night eating on the mud flats. Anybody who has kept ducks will know that the last statement was not wholly accurate. If there is food on the stubbles, the ducks will eat it. They don't really have the capacity to ignore food; I have known them eat so much they cannot get themselves into the air. They crash along the ground flapping their wings, trying to get airborne. I think this must be pollution of their blood with domestic ducks, which cannot fly; wild Mallard drakes are particularly promiscuous and almost like Vikings come into domestic duck ponds, pillaging food and raping the females.

This morning there are hundreds of them, flying up from Calshot and Marchwood. The banana ships dump great loads of any fruit that is going rotten into the creeks on the opposite side of the estuary to their unloading wharves. This keeps the ducks down river until the tide is almost full, feasting on the soft fruit. When they do fly upstream, they come in great long skeins, long chevrons of ducks stretching back for half a mile or more. There are so many, that even passing over at two or three hundred feet, the whistle of their pinion feathers comes down sharp and clear in the quiet of the early morning.

Wandering vaguely about in the quiet, quite suddenly it occurs that today is Sunday. There is no traffic on the roads, Southampton lies in slumber on this wonderful summer morning. When there is a major project on-going on the farm – silage, haymaking, drilling or harvest – it is very easy to lose track of what day of the week it is. One day runs into the next, especially if the situation demands working right through the night.

The kitchen exudes its special welcome; it takes you gently into itself, holding you warm. The gentle heat from the Aga, the beating heart of the home, beckons to you, pulling you to its towel rail, which really is the most sought-after seat in the house. The clock on the wall has a single electronic 'tick', there is no 'tock'; it is nearly half past five, it also tells me that first high water is but twenty minutes away. What salmon and sea trout that come up on this tide will be in Testwood pool by now. The grey mullet will be poking around the reed islands picking up any food that they find. They are great barrel-shaped fish, solid and firm, good to eat and, caught on a rod, magnificent fighters.

Upstairs to bed; but for my swim in the river I would be weary. The room isn't really mine anymore; it smells of female potions. The dressing table has been swamped with strange-shaped bottles, different combs and brushes have pushed my single brush and comb to one side.

A perfectly sculpted calf and foot showed at the side. The sheet covering the flame-haired beauty in bed. The calf ivory-coloured, the foot pinkish with freckles, where the sun had invaded through the sandals she had been wearing. She lay breathing deeply; a woman's sleep has depth and peace just after dawn, and, beside her, the scent of her hair heavy in the nose, asleep in seconds.

CHAPTER EIGHT
(August)

The back end of summer dawdles idly into autumn; this is a wonderful time of the year when the summer weather hangs on. The deeper-rooted trees like oak still look green, but it is a tired sort of green. The beeches up on the chalk are changing colour by the hour, from yellow to red and then to brown. The beech woods are carpeted with the fallen nuts, which scrunch under the feet of your horse. The ride-ways are under a tide of crisp brown leaves, beautiful in their own right, set off against the last of the foxgloves, whose spire-like flower are alive with bees.

This year there more pink and white flower spires than I have ever seen; is this the long hot, dry summer, or crossbreeds from gardens or lately the Garden Centres springing up everywhere?

The river is just bearable to swim in. The first plunge into the water takes your breath away, but to swim amongst the late run sea trout is a privilege not granted to many. They are sulky at the moment, because of the weather, but when the moon starts to wane, they will offer sport through the night and the cold dawns of autumn.

What autumn-flushed grass there was, is dying back through lack of rain, but there must be something in it, as the dairy cows eat it with relish. Their coats glow with health and they begin to get that sort of dappled spotting like circus horses. Is this the dry matter in the grass, one wonders, or the minerals and trace elements they pick up in the soil on the roots? Certainly, I have seen a dairy cow scoffing dry earth, especially if they have been ill and shut in. We can produce a mineral mix whose spectrum would seem to cover every need, but it never does. Through the year the cattle have unlimited access to blocks, tube and liquid mineral additives, but they do not impart the dappled effect of wonderful health that their own earth gives them, tearing it up with their tongues with the roots attached.

Take the time to watch a cow graze; they have no top teeth in the front of their jaw, but rather a hard plate, so their bottom teeth trap the grass on this, and they pull rather than bite. When the grass is young and longer, they wrapped their tongue around it and pull, tearing great wads of it up. They stand and eat a half circle, then step forward again eating the next half circle, swallowing the grass so that they fill their stomachs quickly. The grass is broken down by stomach acid; as this happens, they tend to lie down, bringing up the half-digested grass to chew it again, this time thoroughly.

This is known as 'cudding' or 'chewing the cud', the cud being the semi-digested grass. It is important that this natural thing is not disturbed; they, the cattle, will lie down, look dreamily at the horizon and chew. They not only chew, but they belch and fart, and low across the meadow the smell of milky breath lies sweet. The lumps of cud can be seen travelling back up their digestive tract, as the cattle almost heave for them. They look about as big as a tennis ball, but I cannot say for certain – I've never had a cow willing to let me have one to study.

All types of grazing animals, graze in different ways. The black and white films about the 'Old West' where the cattleman hates the sheep farmer are based on fact. As I have already written, cattle pull the grass, sheep nibble it down to its growing point, and with some of the prairie grasses this killed it for that year. Couple this with the fact that cattle will not follow sheep in grazing, and perhaps you can see why the cattlemen used to make war on the sheep farmers. Where the sheep had been there was no grass for the cattle to graze.

Horses are said to be the 'ruination' of any good pasture – not strictly true, but one can see where the saying comes from. Horses like the 'grass that grew last night', in other words the freshly grown growth. They leave the rest, which results in the sward becoming patchy and growing in clumps. If the pasture was topped*[43] weekly this would not happen and the grazing horses would eat more of the grass and consequently be cheaper to keep. Horses will follow cattle on a grazing sward and vice versa, but horses do not relish following sheep.

It is unwise to let cattle or horses attempt to follow sheep. They will get infected with worms from the sheep and probably keds and ticks. The most industrious of farm animals, that most intelligent, that most accommodating, that most handsome of animals and of course the cleanest – I write of course of the domestic pig, if given the chance an efficient grazing animal. They are wonderful cleaners of a field; watch and look when passing an outdoor pig herd. They leave nothing, they root out roots when they have eaten the top growth: couch rhizomes, dock, brambles, they are all the same to the pig, out they come to be eaten. Of course it all looks a little like the Somme battlefield, so plough it before the pigs are moved out. They will go through every cubic inch of the soil, looking for roots.

Strip graze them over swedes and kale. Then follow in with the field spring wheat, which will make the flourmill manager salivate, whilst looking at its quality. He will want it badly, badly enough to pay well over the odds for it, so make him. Five tons of best bread-making wheat would not cover the cost of the suit he wears.

The surface of the stubble fields is like concrete, hard and very dusty; if a Land Rover goes past it is wreathed in dust, a vortex of spinning dust flies out between the rear wheels. We should be ploughing ready for the autumn drilling, but the ground is too hard. We would force the issue with the two big Massey-Ferguson's but the strain put on the stubble busters would be enormous. We tried up the north end of the farm. The busters' tines went in, the tractors exhaust bellowed and threw out black smoke, the tractor reared like a hard-pushed horse … so we gave up.

The only ploughing we can get done is the grass leys due to come up. The soil beneath the grass roots is workable, because it has just a little dampness in it. If, however, we plough it and no rain comes we will have achieved nothing. The furrows will dry along with the organic matter, which may well blow away. When in doubt, the best thing perhaps is to do nothing. This is generally the best course of non-action.

Instead, on this day I drive up to see a friend, who farms around Marlborough in Pewsey Vale. This is real down land, great rolling hills of chalk with huge areas of flat land between them. The soil is light puffy chalk, which seems to grow anything except heather and birch trees; because of this, like the Berkshire Ridgeway, it is one of my favourite places on earth. Up through Salisbury, Amesbury, Upavon on the east side of Salisbury Plain and thence across to Alton Priors.

Simon farms around Milk Hill under the watchful gaze of the Pewsey Vale white horse. There are lots of tiny hamlets with magical names and magical dwellings, names like All Cannings, Stanton St Bernard and Honeystreet to name a few. The downs are steep, with sheep walks around them; even they have more sense than to make a direct line to the summits. They come at the summit obliquely, or around and around, gradually making height. In between the huge hummocks of the downs, there are flat areas, fields of hundreds of acres running from Alton Barnes to East Kennett.

We have had a few hare-coursing meetings there with the Saluki Club. The hares were exceptional, in fact the best hares I have ever known for fitness. They have to have speed and stamina to live at Milk Hill. There is barely any cover in the coursing season, autumn and winter, so they rely on speed and agility to escape the dogs. In three meetings we actually killed one, which was great. Professional hare coursing is not about killing hares, which is hard for non-country people to understand. Two dogs are matched against each other, using a live hare, in no-way fettered, pushed up by beaters on the hare's own ground and given 'law'.

I have written about 'law' earlier in this book. 'Law' is giving the quarry enough advantage over the dogs so they are very seldom actually caught. We do not want them caught – understand that if you can! If you kill the hares, they will not be there for the next meeting. The winner of a course, two dogs slipped on a hare, is judged to be the dog that did most work before the hare escapes.

Salukis, like other running dogs, are 'sighted hounds'. They hunt by sight, not scent. They can obviously run faster than hares ... but they are not so agile. A hare can turn and dodge much quicker than a Saluki. It is the same for the other sight hounds – greyhounds (the fastest of them all), deerhounds, Borzoi and we had better add whippet. They are sight hounds, but rarely get to terms with a hare. The whippet people will argue, but the fact is they don't. I have 'slipped' some whippet meetings as the 'slipper'.

Let me explain. When a hare is beaten up, the slippers 'shy'. The slipper has a special slip lead – two collars that are released simultaneously when the two dogs are sighted onto the hare. When the slipper judges that sufficient law has been given, he pulls the inner lead, which opens the two collars and the dogs are coursing. I always gave the hare eighty yards of law with whippets. They are very quick off the mark, but don't have much stamina; they are up with the hare, which quickly jinks away; first dog up to affect the hare turning, three points. The hare quickly realises that the whippets can turn as quickly as she can. There lies the danger for her, so she changes up a gear and is gone.

Sure, whippets can catch and kill hares, if the hare is not given law, but a collie or Springer spaniel can do that. That is just hare killing, not hare coursing; a very ancient sport going back into pre-history, with the rules. Simon was suffering badly from the M4 corridor. Their previously beautiful hamlets, lived in by the indigenous people of the area, now had become 'a sought-after village' in estate agent speak, the same as in Hampshire. The place was filling up 'with undesirables', i.e. townies with aspirations to become country dwellers, very few of whom you would want to pass the time of day with.

Watch them in the pub on Sundays, watch them 'in their cups' and you will quickly see what they are, ill-mannered British louts, ex-Saturday night binge drinkers and those, I might add, are the females. Simon, a long-time friend, wanted to know how we kept them at bay, stopped them wandering everywhere over the farm, driving down made-up farm tracks. The next-door farm to him had just had a fatality: a herd of beef bullocks had trampled a female walker, who despite being warned several times, had insisted on walking her dog along a footpath in the bullocks' field. It was a footpath, therefore she had 'every right' to be there.

Ho hum, you cannot put sense where sense does not belong. The cattle came after the dog, which was on a lead, the walker did not have the experience to let the dog go, she just got in the way and was killed by trampling hooves. This happens every year, people get killed or maimed by cattle. They sometimes think that because there is a public footpath, the field somehow becomes theirs. The public paths have been there for generations, to allow people to walk from one village to another by the shortest route. It does not mean that the farmer cannot keep stock in them, he has to.

If you choose to walk in the country, you should make yourself aware of the inherent dangers and avoid them, not tempt them on a point of mistaken 'rights'. A footpath is just that, it does not mean you can walk along it and let your dog or children run anywhere out of control.

There was a rather pretty Welsh lady living in the town; she was told times enough to keep her dog under control, but she informed me very tartly that 'Owen', her Corgi, was a cattle dog, quite capable of looking after himself. Corgis, if I didn't know, were used by drovers to herd cattle. This she added in a tone that intimated I was stupid. Now dairy Shorthorns are the softest animals I know, or at least ours were, great red roan lumbering animals. They knew about dogs, as Frank the dairyman had collies, three of them, sharp-witted, sharp-toothed dogs that could see a kick coming.

The poor Corgi, Owen, could not, and when it came it hit the dog in the side of the head, a blow that must have turned his brain to porridge. Owen arched over backwards, landing on his side; he got shakily on his feet, took three steps, collapsed, going into spasm, then died. Any hope of a casual dalliance I might have had about with his mistress died with Owen.

There are those incomers who are a blessing, when a village gets itself into the Sunday glossy section. Change is inevitable. The usual sequence of events are such: enquiries about the 'much sought-after village' are filed, and every time a house/cottage comes on the market it is offered to the town people, as country people cannot compete financially. Nor do they get the chance; the dwelling is sold without its coming onto the open market. The first big silver German car arrives in the village, intelligence about the newcomers is gleaned from the first person to go and 'do' for the newcomers. The female is amazed how little her first 'char' costs. This, after all, is Wiltshire not Kensington.

It is the same with the children's ponies: they are purchased, then taken to live in a tiny paddock, being stabled in single-skin buildings in one of the coldest areas of Southern England. However, they are soon co-opted into the Pony Club, where someone who knows about ponies and horses can keep an eye on the animals. The children become 'first-generation Pony Club' children, a term of abuse, scorn and sarcasm. Within a few years half the dwellings in the village have the obligatory large German car parked on its front garden.

The village is now two villages almost. There are the 'villagers', the original inhabitants, or what is left of them, and the incomers who are not nor ever will be 'village' people, because they do not think like village people. The village shop closes with only half the village using it because the incomers do their shopping in Marlborough. The village school closes because the incomers send their children elsewhere, so that they can complain about how much they are spending on their children's education – and this is happening all over rural England. It is the slow death of our countryside that we are watching!

The village, Simon declared, had become like East and West Berlin, and only the arrival of a farmer's daughter, an ex-London doctor, seemed able and willing to bridge the gap. Simon listened to the story of the Old Basing farmer. Would that be worth a try perhaps? I explained that we were lucky we had no footpaths over home, Devon or Hampshire. We had tried the 'Let's be accommodating approach', but it would require special insurance to cover it.

If somebody fell in the hatch pool and drowned it would be deemed to be our fault. So we went the other way, a robust approach to trespass, impounding cars by blocking them in and other anti-social measures. We allowed horse riders over on designated rides, but they had to sign an insurance waiver, drawn up by the insurance company itself. The theory was that young lady riders would never put their horses in harm's way, and also they became more sets of eyes looking out for ne'er do wells. It worked for us, so I hoped it would work for Simon.

To an outsider, it must seem entirely unreasonable for a farmer to eject somebody from his property, when it is patently obvious that the trespasser is doing absolutely no harm at all. The problem is that a trespasser has to be checked on; from half a mile away the farmer cannot be sure who it is. The amount of equipment stolen these days beggar's belief: small stuff mainly, batteries from tractors, combines etc. Chainsaws left in the back of a Land Rover are considered to be fair game, and a legitimate prize by our friends from the caravan park.

I am told, however, that tractors now go missing, and just two years ago we had fertiliser stolen, half a lorry load in fact. It is increasingly difficult to keep things secure; gates on all the entrances have to be locked overnight. Complex electronic alarms and movement detectors have to be installed, equipment permanently marked and now, for goodness sake, the animals have to be electronically micro-chipped in case they get stolen.

Courting couples can give us amusement and the couple embarrassment if they happen to be parked up somewhere quiet, getting to know each other and the final gate is locked. From the house windows it is always apparent when somebody has spent too long parked up – they fly around the farm lanes like a bee caught in a bottle, getting ever more panicky. The headlights of their vehicle charting their progress, it is rather satisfying to think if they cannot get out, then nobody can get in.
Eventually, they have to be let out, they look shamefaced and awkward mainly; some are truculent and aggressive, generally the ones not with their rightful companion.

The summertime courting couples are not too much of a problem. They park up if the weather is fine, leave their vehicle and wander into a copse or long grass. Only when they drive onto muddy tracks and get stuck do they become a nuisance, because we have to pull them out.

From this you can judge we try at least to be fair; the nuisance factor is the problem, stopping what you are doing, to go and see what the vehicle or person was who was heading towards the farmyards. A large white van or a black Japanese pick-up truck sets the alarm bells ringing. Tarmac people, scrap-iron dealers, they do anything to get onto the farms and have a good look round, to return later and steal some of what they saw. Red diesel and central heating fuel seem to be the 'in' booty at the moment; as we counter one move of theirs, they come up with another wheeze.

CHAPTER NINE
(September)

The glass*[44] had fallen in a spectacular way over the day despite there not being a breath of wind or a cloud in the sky. From thirty-one inches of mercury to a little over twenty-eight inches was not unheard of, but the weather was, it seemed, going to break with some violence. Through no fault of their making, we were currently lodging three of the stable girls who helped look after the horses living in our stables. They belonged to a young lady who had another yard not far away. Though not anything to do with our family, we none the less kept an eye on them. With the weather on the change it was suggested that the animals should be brought in for the night, 'to be on the safe side'.

Throughout the morning the recently emptied covered yards of the dairies were refilled with straw. What was feared most was the extreme thunderstorms that could afflict the area. The cattle would seek shelter beneath the trees and if the tree was struck, cattle died. It seemed to be airless outside; still the sky was cloudless, but the most gentle breeze blew from the south. More convinced by this, the horses were brought in, despite protests from the head girl, who became petulant and short with me.

They were fed extra hay and greens from the cattle food; they would not starve. Fifteen horses loose in a field when things were quiet would be okay, but if one gets spooky, the rest will follow.

Over tea the girls began to tease, making a big thing of getting up from the table, going to the window and pronouncing it to be 'not raining yet'. They were not average stable girls; two of the three had already won places at the Royal Veterinary College and were here to learn more practical skills. The other girl, Lesley, was having her own yard in about a year; her wealthy parents were actively looking for such a property, 'somewhere near the sea'.

Having the horses in had curtailed the girls' movements somewhat; used in the winter to having the horses indoors, they seldom went anywhere, having to always feed them a late meal. In the summer they made up for this by going out in the evenings, cinema, theatre or to the Agricultural College if there was a visiting vet lecturing. Lesley had forgotten her petulance and came with the other two and myself to feed the ducks. We watched them flighting in for some time before Charlotte spotted an unusual light flickering on the horizon, well beyond the Isle of Wight.

None of the girls had been in the area long enough to have witnessed the extreme electrical storms the area suffered, about one year in seven. They watched the ducks for a little while longer, counting how many in ten minutes and games such as this, until Lesley whispered, awestruck, 'God in Heaven! That's lightning!'

They drove gently back to the house; as they fed the horses they could hear a distant continuous rumble, one or two spots of rain landed with a ping on the Land Rover bonnet. They stayed whole, proud, the dusty bonnet holding their shape. The next spots were like a handful of heavy shot hitting the vehicle, a short drum roll on the canvas tilt. The air now was heavy and hot, so close as to be uncomfortable. I sent the girls indoors; to hide their fear Jane suggested they race. Nobody could tell us why that, when there was an electrical storm, the telephone tinkled happily; told not to touch it until the approaching storm had passed, the girls sat at the kitchen table, white faced and silent. Charlotte, whose red-head skin was almost translucent on the best of days, looked paler than ever, her eyes like a startled rabbit.

They heard a loud click, the kitchen was filled with white and purple light, the electric lights went out. The click was the main fuse tripping. The thunder was all around them. The windows rattled; the very air smelt burnt. I smiled in the dark, remarking that it was 'raining outside'. Their screams of terror became screams of laughter. The storm seemed reluctant to move away; for an hour it rumbled around our part of the valley, until everyone was tired.

The rain was heavy, intermittent and made the air smell of damp earth, but it was very welcome. Tomorrow, the river would be brown, all the dust on the harvest fields would be washed gently down the tracks, through the land drains; it had seemed that each wheat stalk, still proud of the soil, was coated in dust, caught there by the tiny spiders' webs, which are normally covered in the dew. Dirty gossamer strands hanging on hedgerows would be washed down, to join the silty grey-brown rush of water heading for the river. Now it is a question of how much water is going to come down the river. The tide is on the ebb at the moment, at least it will be daylight before there is anything of a problem.

Another great flash and hiss of lightning, a crash of falling timber along with the crack and roar of thunder, the rain rattled against the windows. Then quiet; this particular storm moved north. Taking the opportunity the electrical trip switch was pushed shut. The lights came on again, steady, not flickering. They were powered by a turbine in the mill on the river. Only when I saw them in the light, did I realise how terrified the three girls had been; because of this I offered to do the horses. The animals' only concern it seemed was whether anyone was coming to feed them; the storm had not worried them at all.

The crash of falling timber we had heard from indoors was a huge old ash tree; it had butt rot*45 we knew, so its complete collapse through a lightning strike was no surprise. It had come down, straddling the top feeder stream, but had not done any significant damage. To be quite honest I had not noticed that the town lay in darkness; also, the normal glow in the sky that was Southampton at night as far as we were concerned was not showing. It wasn't a surprise therefore when the head of maintenance at the town hospital pulled into the house yard, begging to borrow the grain-store generator. He was a splendid chap, labouring under a maintenance manager who knew nothing. Three times he had purchased for the hospital a 'suitable' generator; three times it had failed the course. In his defence the manager did have rather a good degree in history of art, which I'm sure stood him in good stead.

The grain-store generator was mounted on the chassis of a Bedford T. K. lorry; originally from a coaster, Carl the engineer had made it fully mobile. It was no problem therefore to get it to the hospital; leaving a message for Charlotte to come and retrieve me, I left with the hospital maintenance man for the grain dryer.

The sky was still full of cloud, but the rain that we had was nothing much really; it had sounded a lot, being in short and heavy bursts. The lanes were not in any way awash. The horse chestnuts, which seems to be suffering most through lack of rain, had cast down bunches of leaves, which always seemed to land underside up, pale almost white in the headlights. There were the usual twigs and small branches that heavy rain would normally knock down strewn along the lanes. The lorry tyres crushed them, along with the tons of acorns that now lay like a mosaic of brown, green and white marbles, shiny and wet. The gamekeepers would now be driven to distraction by the pheasants that would come to feed on the crushed acorns. In the normal course of events, if the pheasants were not visible to passing traffic, nobody thought much about them, but 'track rod' poaching becomes very rife, if they are spread all over the roads and lanes.

Good, wonderful steady rain began to fall at about three the next morning; it didn't blow, it didn't hammer up against the bedroom windows like spent shot, it just fell gently from the sky, life giving, luscious and sweet. Outside in the fields and meadows, the mist would be smoking up from the warm earth, to form itself into layers, only to reluctantly burn away if the sun showed itself at dawn. There is always something very comforting about lying in bed, listening to the rain and being able to distinguish the various trickles, gurgles and murmurings from the drains and home gutters, listening to the top feeder stream at the head of the garden, now cascading over the sluice, washing the detritus of a dry summer away.

With the light came the excited family noises of the moorhens, bossy and urgent, unlike the last of house martins, still hanging on to the hope perhaps of not having to fly to Durban. I don't know what they were thinking, except on that particular morning they were not getting up.

The rain had altered everything. That ultimate, joyous act of faith could happen: autumn sowing. Granted we were perhaps two weeks late overall, but that would be made up quickly. Everything was ready, machinery up to the top line, trailers loaded with seed and compound*[46] fertiliser. The game was never to be held up because the sowing had caught up with the ploughs. Seven tractors started the ploughing, five of our own, plus two contractors'. Each pulling twelve reversible ploughs, together they turned over land of forty-two yards; it had to be got on with but not rushed or slapdash, as nothing following can make up for bad ploughing.

With our soil types, the next things on the plough are disc-harrows; these chop the furrows into small pieces. After some years on stubble they are not needed for this initial breaking up, but this year because of the dry time they were needed to break up the hard-packed soil. After the discs came the spring tine harrows, lighter raking machines to break the soil into smaller lumps. Not too small though – winter sown cereals need a fairly knobbly tilth, to let the young shoots shelter from the wind. They would break down soon enough with the weather; if the seedbed was made too fine, the rain might make it 'cap off', that is, settle the surface into an impenetrable crust. There was no rolling; spring cereals are rolled to conserve the moisture in the soil and given an average year there would be plenty of moisture coming in next few months.

We have three types of soil on the farm. Each one needs different treatment. The top ground is the start of the chalk escarpment. It is rather lovely; it smells sweet and fresh, grows average to good crops and presents fewest problems. It also grows wonderful flints; we say 'grows', because a field can be cleared of them, the next year there will be less, but there are flints where two years ago there were not any. See if you can work this one out: for at least four hundred years this area has produced flint, some big, some small, and from this flint has come the foundation of most of the buildings, our living house, roadways and yards. The escarpment does not get any lower, the flints keep coming and being removed; we say they grow, and even in the twenty-first century, we are glad of them, as a better foundation for a road would be hard to find.

The second soil type is what is called alluvial soil, that which is left by the river or has been left by the river in conjunction with the tide. It is wonderful growing soil, easy to work, inherently fertile, holds its moisture fairly well, and goes rank and smelly if not kept well drained.

Lastly there is this same soil, lying over what must have been the shore of a bay, a long gravel spit up to eighteen inches down. This gravel spit packs down like concrete. The Abbey is built on it and that hasn't shifted for the better part of a thousand years. This has to be broken up every other year at least, better every year in fact, because if not it lays foetid, wet and dank, and would hardly produce a single ton of wheat to the acre. Treat it right. Sub-soiled vigorously, it will produce three tons to the acre. An old farm map has the bottom side of this land marked down as 'The Snipe Marsh', with drawings of flying snipe and rushes. That was when the rain water flowed over the gravel spit and emptied, or rather bubbled, into four acres at the bottom end.

Running east to west is a 'French Drain'*[47]; someone in desperation thought that it would work and keep the bottom end dry. There was far too much water running off from two hundred and fifty acres for that to happen. Now this works as long as not too much water arrives at once; it's better to break up the gravel spit with a sub-soil so that more water filters down through the gravel layer, where it eventually creeps into the river.

It was fairly certain that most of the rain had 'gone in'; the first storm that had arrived had run over the surface of the land and escaped. The rain now, the steady rain that had started in the early hours, was being sucked into the dry earth. The air seemed cleaner, washed now in fact, as the farm vehicles for weeks had been churning up dust. At first the buildings themselves seemed to be made of mud. A thin layer covered everything, but as the morning progressed surfaces again showed their true colour, as the rain sluiced down over them.

Ploughing was now going on apace; at first the tractor exhausts bellowed, and smoke in a continuous plume followed them across the fields. Then as the land freed itself up in the steady rain, it became easier, the huge chunks of hardened earth that ran away in front of the shares, gradually stopped appearing, furrows straighter than a bullet's flight formed. The tractors' breath smelt less, the engines ran smoother now, the governors not teased into offering more fuel because of the hard-packed earth.

By three that afternoon, seed wheat and fertiliser were rattling down through the combine drills, placing the seed in rows. It had stopped raining and the air was filled with the smell of warm earth. There were no rooks or gulls; they knew that the recently dry earth would not yield any grubs or worms, and they would have to wait a few days for them to get back into the damp layers. The rear tyres of the tractors were not picking up any soil, their huge cleats remained clean, biting into the earth, giving the traction to haul the massive ploughs. In thirty years there had been such wonderful improvements in the modern tractor. Harry Ferguson's three-point linkage and inbuilt hydraulic system had seen to that. They were comfortable, powerful but balanced machines, even on the delicate soil structure of the water meadows; despite their weight, the modern Massey-Ferguson's skipped over the soft ground, without tearing it to pieces.

This autumn I was allocated a ninety-horse Fergie, four-wheel drive pulling a six-furrow non-reversible plough, the plough bodies of which were so thin through wear, that I used the rear of one to cut some string. The rest of the plough was in good order. The beams were straight, the adjustments worked smoothly, but I felt certain that as soon as the discolouration was worn from the bodies, they would collapse. I was to plough the two hundred and fifty acres that had the gravel pan underneath; the sub-soiler had already been through it so it was a tangle of broken earth, ruts and at that moment dust and stones.

I did not mind, I was the owner's grandson, and as such was expected to take on the horrible jobs and make a proper fist of it. These particular fields I had learnt to plough in, how it was set out, where the bad bits were; my tractor in those days was generally the fourth in line ploughing. The tractors we had were twenty-odd horsepower, rear-wheel drive with two furrows being pulled. The tractors had no cabs either, so the driver was very much out in the elements. A 'West of England' wheat sack, hung and tied down each side of the bonnet, directed the warm air from the engine back onto the driver.

Luxury? Of course it was! Better than walking behind a pair of horses mile after mile, one foot in the furrow and the other on the ridge. Little grey Fergies didn't spend their time farting in your face either; only artists and poets eulogise over ploughing with horses, that's because they never had to do it. For my part I have ploughed five turns with horses at a Steam Fair, you know the sort of thing, roughly one thousand yards on almost flat ground. The grass in the area was like a lawn, cut short with a forage harvester. I wanted to say that I had ploughed with horses. The next day I knew I had ploughed with horses. I won a prize for my efforts, but hardly had the strength to walk up and collect it, every bone in my body aching like the devil.

Three days into my ploughing stint one of the bodies fell in half. Together with the farm mechanic I welded it back together. The next day another lost a large lump from its trailing edge; it didn't make that much difference so I carried on. Eventually there was, I judged, another half an hour's ploughing to complete the job; gentle though I had been with the plough, one complete body cracked away from its backing plate, falling under the plough behind. It ripped that one off its plate, the bolts pulling away from the body. It was practically lunchtime, so while the others stopped for lunch, I made two passes with one of the reversible ploughs to finish. It had become a matter of pride to finish the job; it didn't look too bad despite the furrows collapsing the whole time. One pass with the disc harrows and the field would be fit to drill.

The cereals being sown were milling wheat, feed wheat, feed barley and oats. The cultivations and sowing went on sometimes until ten at night. This did not make us that popular in the immediate area. But the afternoon came when we could say we had finished. The farm manager and mechanic had planned a secret party. Everybody was bidden back to the house to celebrate the end of sowing and catching up the time we had lost. Speeches were made about the quality of the work done, the way the machinery had never 'missed a beat' which allowed the work to progress without a hold-up. This was down to Carl the farm mechanic, a German who kept every machine in tip-top condition. Now sowing was done with, Carl would have the machines used serviced in his workshop. Nothing was skimped. Embarrassed admittance that my efforts with a worn-out plough was a joke: the plough was meant to collapse within an hour, but the joke had turned against them. Now it was time enough to relax.

We country people call them 'field sports', the BBC, ITV, Channel Four et al call them 'blood sports'. Our various organisations have asked them not to do so, but having found a raw spot, the television people carry on with 'blood sports' and take every opportunity to show the country people as cruel, wicked, barbarous people. You can lay before them facts about the decline of our bird of population, which the RSPB wave away and dismiss as wrong. We see what is happening because we live in the country. This counts for nothing.

At the moment the west side of this country is fighting against TB in our farm animals, costing heartache and millions of pounds. We have known, as have our vets, that it is the huge badger population spreading it. We need to have a thin-out of the badgers – kill them, that is. The genuine farmer on the BBC's 'Country File', Adam Henson, said this; now the Animal Rights people are threatening to 'burn his children'. This is just two of the idiocies we labour under; is it any wonder the main of country people despise 'townies'?

I am about to write about how we country people relax, spend our leisure time, enjoy each other's company, converse about things that matter. I am going to write about field sports.

Because the autumn sowing was late this year, September was taken up with work. The land was barely workable where cereals had been grown this year, so it was only where the grass leys were being ploughed that we could progress.

CHAPTER TEN
(October)

Partridge shooting, which starts in September, rather went by the board, but now we could start with an easy conscience, as the work had been done. At the start of this book, I wrote about Charles 'Turnip' Townsend, who introduced turnips into crop rotation; this made the country an exporter of wool, quality wool from the backs of the sheep that had to eat the turnips. Another benefit was that turnips growing in fields gave shelter and cover for grey partridges, so they increased dramatically. Partridge had always been the preferred quarry species of the sportsman, pheasants came much later; the birds were shot over Pointers though, not driven over a line of waiting guns by beaters. Pointers, air-scenting dogs as opposed to ground-scenting dogs (mud snuffling dogs e.g. spaniels and Labradors), were cast forward either by the 'guns'*[48] into the wind, or by professional dog handlers employed by the guns.

The Pointers would find and point. The guns would move to the pointing dogs, the game would be 'flushed'*[49] and hopefully shot. This style of shooting is still used today, generally referred to as 'walked-up game', carried out by people who are sometimes referred to as 'purists', that is, saying a more natural way to present the quarry.

'Driven partridge' shooting employs beaters. The birds are flushed over guns lined out under the flight lines. The old-fashioned name is a 'battue' and the idea came from the Continent. The guns are spaced out forty to fifty yards apart on 'pegs' which the keeper has set out; at a given signal the beaters move forward, slowly flushing the birds forward over the guns. These days behind the guns are the professional dog people, the 'pickers up' – the people who 'mark down' the shot birds and when the drive or battue is over, they send their dogs out to collect find and retrieve them. I must own up to the fact that of the two systems of shooting partridge, I much prefer shooting over Pointers. I treasure the partnership I have with my Pointer, the way she thinks with me. There are, however, very few grey partridge shoots running in this country these days. The skills required have largely died away.

Having or owning a shoot these days is an extremely expensive pastime; if it can be worked in with normal farming practice, with perhaps a tractor driver mad keen to help, it can work. I know of a pheasant shoot where the farm secretary does most of the vermin control and feeding. A very glamorous young lady, who loves shooting and hunting, she also owns some very good Labrador Retrievers.

Some estates have gone wholly commercial, that is, shooting has become a large income source. The shooting is let to visiting syndicates on let days. That is, they book and pay for a day's shooting, for say between eight and ten guns, for an agreed number of birds. Into this world the French partridge, or red-legged partridge, has arrived. They are easier to rear artificially than grey partridge, lend themselves to a greater stocking density and are more sedentary than their English cousins – that is they stay at home. They fly well, but not as well as the greys. They are perhaps more robust in that a spell of bad weather they seem to shrug it off better, but I have to ask myself: are they truly wild?

In Devon we live close to a commercial shoot, which rears French partridge in some numbers. They are colourful birds, which hang around the farm buildings or the garden. They seem as tame as reared pheasants, barely bothering to avoid humans. The initial driving of them over a line of guns seems to be a problem. They are reluctant to rise and fly, rather they like to skulk along on the ground, running.

The invitation had been on the kitchen mirror for about three months; big shooting estates, as is the one next door, have all their shooting planned before the grouse season starts on the 12th August. It was very flattering not to be invited to the first day, the partridges would have been a little green and wayward. The shoot is now just two days away and some rust and cobwebs needed to be done away with. A visit to Apsely Shooting School was quickly arranged, where David Olive's expertise and laughter would make a pleasant start to a relaxing few days. Charlotte had been keen to start shooting so she had the last lesson of the day, shooting a twenty bore; the gun was a present for my fourteenth birthday, and now fitted her rather better than it did me. My lesson was quickly done with, and rather than prolong the waiting for Charlotte, I asked David to let her have a longer session.

Claiming I had something to get in Andover, I left her to it. In fact I drove around the back of the School to watch her shoot, so that she was thinking more of what she was doing and not shooting for my sake. Shooting, done properly, taught properly, is a little like riding a horse – once learnt you never forget how. Charlotte had not touched a gun since last February, but she came back to it easily. When I picked her up she was animated and happy; she had in truth shot more than rather well. I like to see females shoot, and love to see them on the shooting field. The men behave so much better in their presence.

Two or three days off would refresh the mind, I felt, and along with some of the other farm staff, that's what I determined to do.
The invitation to shoot partridges had come from a 'Partridge Manor'*[50] in the north of the county, in an area known as the Candovers. Either myself or my grandfather shot there; in exchange the hosts came to 'flight duck'*[51] later in the year.

After checking that everything was under control with the stable girls, I wandered down to the workshop to let Carl know I was off the place. It was strange being alone, driving to a day's shooting. I liked shooting well enough. The love I have for the company, the area I was shooting in on this particular day, the chalk downland was more than strong.

Once onto the Arlesford road heading towards Alton, the country changed; there were trees growing here, mainly beech, great stately green towers in the summer, now going back to copper and gold as the autumn arrived. The farms had mainly finished their sowing, though there were still rows of combined straw across some fields. Extra cover for pheasants perhaps, something to dive under if danger threatened.

Though this road was now a new dual carriageway, with huge wide verges, it was obvious the local wildlife had not got used to the increased speed of the traffic. There were several dead pheasants at the edge of the tarmac surface and some ground into it, flattened into a thin sheet of feathers.Normally these corpses would be attracting crows and magpies, but here there were none, so one can assume the local gamekeepers were up to speed on vermin control.

At the top of the hill, away to my right, there was not a cow, bullock or heifer in sight. I could see for miles. There were a few sheep, but the main of the land was down to cereal. Agriculture was defining its areas even more so with the growth of the nation's infrastructure.
It had been a gradual almost unseen change, until it was suddenly there: how did that happen? Up until the mid sixties it was a strange farm that didn't have at least some cattle, leaving aside the pig and poultry farms. They went more specific a decade earlier.
Now the West Country is referred to as the main area of dairy

farms, along with Cheshire – both areas of more assured higher rainfall.

Imagine the change in lifestyle for a farmer and his family if he sells his milking cows. The drudgery of what used to be called 'tied to a cow's tail' is suddenly gone. No more leaving a warm bed at four thirty, five o'clock on wet and freezing February mornings.

The Land Rover tyres sing along the newly laid tarmac. As we run downwards towards the town of Arlesford, the trees are evident again, oaks, alder, poplar, we are in the valley of the River Arle. Over the back of the town, in what wet meadows there are, peewits wheel about the sky, as a man and tractor feed bullocks in an area of rich grassland by the river. The River Arle is a tributary of the River Itchen, which runs through Winchester, a famous chalk stream which eventually joins the River Test in Southampton Water.

Turn left at the Broadway, a wide street where the sheep fairs take place – a mention of one shop, Styles, old-fashioned hardware and beautiful ceramics on the left side of Broadway – find somewhere to park and wander down to The Globe for a light breakfast and meet some of the other guns.

The Globe is next to Arlesford Pond – a great understatement, it's a lake of some size, the actual headwaters of the Itchen, put there by some monks who must have had a direct line to their Maker. The dam was built in medieval times to a size we would be hard put to build today, an earth and chalk construction which the B3046 runs over now. On one side is the pond; on the other, a drop of maybe thirty feet, put there by men with wheelbarrows, baskets and horse-drawn carts. That is an act of some faith. The pond is home to countless wildfowl of different sorts and fish, the size of which beggars' belief. The water is chalky, therefore full of food for fish. I promise I have seen carp in there about thirty pounds, and pike, the size of which would make you think twice before swimming there.

Looking over the pub's garden fence at the pond, there seemed to be quite a ripple on the water; the gusty south-westerly would make the shooting harder. The partridge would revel in flying with it. The sky had quite a few high, quickly moving, small clouds, shaped like cauliflower florets; it would rain later, but probably not before dark.

The others of this group had arrived already, and laughed and teased me not just about being late, intimating that Charlotte had delayed me: 'She been laying on your nightshirt?' This was about the most polite jibe. Jamie the vet, Barry the gun-maker, Pat the pilot, all long-time friends, left with me to our host's home. There would be four more guns, who they were we didn't know, but that is part of the joy of a private shoot. The host invites his friends and for me a stranger is a friend you have yet to meet. Part of a good host's duty is to choose eight people who are going to get on together, also knowing them to be safe shots.

There is and seemingly always has been a strict etiquette on behaviour, a bit like going to a hunting meet. Your first duty is to go and say 'Good morning' to your host. This is to let him know you have arrived. Next you must let the head keeper know you have arrived. This is not the time to stand talking to him; he has a lot to do and his hands full. A quick greeting is enough. By now the guns will have introduced themselves to each other if they were not acquainted.

The other four guns on this particular morning were Hamish, another vet, David, a watercress grower, Doctor Spring and John, an agricultural agronomist. We could look forward to some lively conversation over lunch and not a little banter between the vets and the doctor, as is always the way with the two professions.

The guns were called into the very ornate cart shed, where 'pegs were drawn'. This is the drawing of numbers, one to eight, so as to give you your position in the first drive. I drew number two, so the next drive I would be number four peg, moving up two each drive. The host would then let you know the rules for the day: break any of them and you will never be invited again. The statement would probably be something along the lines of: move up two pegs each drive; do not turn around to shoot; no ground game (this estate preserved its brown hares very strictly, anyone taking a shot at one would be sent home immediately, in more than a little disgrace); and shoot safely.

No mention of manners here, the implication was: you are here because we know you have good shooting manners; please do not disappoint us. What are good shooting manners? Something like this: shoot only the birds in your quadrant, do not take shots at the birds heading for the guns alongside you.

Do not take low birds – for half of the drive the beaters will be in your line of sight, like grouse shooting. Peppering a beater with shot will get you banned from all the big estates in the county, Wiltshire and Dorset as well most probably. So make certain what you shoot at is high enough for your shot to be no danger to anyone.

Don't shoot before the 'start' whistle and unload your gun and put it in its sleeve the moment the 'stop' whistle blows, even if at that moment there are half a dozen well-presented partridges heading at you.

During the guns' sojourn in the cart shed, the beaters and keepers had been loaded on the 'beaters cart'*[52] and hauled away to the back of beyond to start driving the partridges over the guns. Along the way, they drop off flankers, older beaters whose job it is to keep the birds flying down the aerial corridor toward the guns. They do this with the use of flags. Flat squares of plastic attached to a stick, the sight and sound of this keep the partridge on line. Well, this is the theory anyway, certainly they make the birds fly much higher as they break sideways. It is a truly horrendous job trying to keep the birds going forward towards the guns, especially when firing starts.

The guns are usually transported to their pegs; suddenly you are standing alone on a windswept hill. The moment of truth. Look to see where the flankers are, where your next-door guns are, finally where the 'pickers up' are behind you. However you deal with your cartridges, do it now; if you load from your pocket, then put some ammunition in there now. If you load from a bag, then make certain it is open and within reach. Personally I load from my right jacket pocket. Thirty rounds in there are enough weight to have on one side of yourself, you need to be relaxed and balanced. Get your gun out of its sleeve, check the bores are clear of obstruction, load both barrels but leave the gun broken, hung over your arm.

Now, you wait until the start whistle blows. These days there are two-way radios to help communications. The start whistle is sounded, the head keeper behind the guns takes a radio message and bids you 'Good shooting' then stands back to watch and appraise. Good luck.

There was one gun to my left, about fifty yards away. The guns to my right were out of my sight around a slight rise and field corner. A hare came cantering past, not hurrying, his soft chestnut and brown fur catching the wind and the light; he was a typical hare of this area, well fed and huge. A rattle of gunshots on my right made the hare check, then stop, he came back past me, not more than a yard from my legs, heading towards a small copse, still not hurrying.

There was a shout, several partridges were flying from my right, turned by the gunshots, crossing in front about forty yards out.

I fired once, bringing down a bird. The others were too tightly packed to shoot. Firing into a bunch is known as 'browning the birds' and is very much frowned upon, birds are wounded that way.

The end of the drive was signalled. I had shot eight birds which the picker-up behind me sent his Labradors to pick. He had a young bitch named Bridey and quite the biggest Lab dog I had ever seen named Zulu; he shone like a guardsman's boot; when he brought back one of the birds, it showed but little in his mouth, he was of tremendous size and a study of canine composure. His owner, Paul, a tall, spare man, was obviously proud of Zulu, which was as it should be.

Lining out for the second drive, I was on number four peg this time. The wind had picked up considerably, tearing the reluctant beech leaves, now brown and gold, from their branches. They came down in great showers, curtains from the highest part of the trees, swirling in circles when they caught the updraft. Each leaf was like an exquisite piece of jewellery, the underside matt copper, the topside a shiny copper as though each one had been polished.
The wind shrieked through the branches of the beech trees, like the wind in the rigging of a ship; the noise drowned out any hope of hearing the start whistle. The keeper in the gun line signalled that the start had been signalled, so we waited.

When the birds came, they were going at extreme speed, very high, so high in fact they did not deviate when they saw the gun line. They had judged it correctly; my total was eight birds again. This time Zulu had to search the woods far behind me. There wasn't a hope of me marking the birds down; the wind had carried them to the far side of the beech brake.

We were driven to the pegs for the next drive. There was a change of plan because of the wind. The birds were going to be flushed out of a field of turnips; they would sit close in this wind then pass over the gun line. The explosive speed of the flushing would make them difficult to hit. This time all the guns could see what was happening. On number six peg for this drive, I was standing in line with a wide ride cut through a stand of Southern beech. This was either the 'hot spot' of the drive, as the birds would tend to fly along this wide ride, or the 'dud peg' where no birds came at all.

It was the former: they wanted, suicidally, to fly along the ride – every bird in my quadrant flew straight at me, as though they were on rails. For two or three minutes I shot quickly, then only took the birds that flew above an imaginary line in the sky; even so I was afraid I may have overdone it just a little. My concern was unwarranted. John and Barry were having some success; along with mine they had just about made the day so far worthwhile.

When asked I plumped for lunch after the fourth drive, which would be the last one. I was told not to hold back; mine host had reckoned on quite a big day. Again we were driving out of turnips, so thank you, Charles Townsend. The wind was very strong now, so strong it was a question of leaning into it to make forward progress. The guns and beaters together faced into the turnips. The beaters went forward, slowly tapping, very gently; the guns remained still. The birds rose, fought for height, then curled back over the beaters; by the time they reached the gun line they were the quickest of the morning. It was a masterly show of partridge driving and exhilarating shooting.

This time I held back just a little; this early in the season there was little point in shooting lots. The farm had to get through November and December, at least showing some partridge in amongst the pheasants. Partridges are much-loved birds by country people; sure we shoot them but not with any intensity somehow. Personally I get sick to death of the gaudy pheasants, parading around the garden crowing and destroying our efforts at horticulture. They are stupid, they never seem to learn where danger is and they are so obviously a foreign import.

I don't spare them; I kill them cleanly using five shot in my twelve or twenty bore. They are an annual harvest like mackerel or herring. Partridges are special, grey partridge that is; they are plump little round birds, brave, good parents, handsome not gaudy and are obviously part of the English landscape. These days partridges are not considered to be the premier game bird, probably because the new breed of shooting people cannot hit them. They are much, much better to eat than pheasants.
Then there is that wonderful rasping call of the cock bird, calling up his family in late summer, as English a sound as a blackbird singing or the twanging ring of a hunting horn early in the morning on cubbing days.

These days I could no more shoot a grey partridge than offer Charlotte up to a white slaver. We had 'shot through', that is to say we did not stop for lunch; when the weather or light is bad in the winter months this often happens. I would always have it so, given the choice. The thought of having to get dressed up after a good shoot lunch, to go out and face the rain or snow again, is not my idea of fun.

Lunch this day was chicken and leek pie, roast potatoes and neeps. The pie was made in great big army dixies – real food. I read the other day of a young lady who went to the Hay-on-Wye Book Festival for the first time. She actually ate some of the canapés – which isn't done at all. They are very funny people, these literary types. The canapés are for show only! A very famous author once said to me: 'Avoid the canapés. They are like eating seagull's shit on biscuits.'

As is so often the case you meet somebody out shooting who becomes over time a close friend. Hampshire people are notoriously reserved. There is a saying that they do not invite you into their home until they have known you five years. Whether this is still true, I don't know. Are there any true-bred Hampshire people these days? I doubt it, because now we travel so widely, work well away from our roots. Just sometimes you meet someone who has an indefinable quality that makes you want him as a friend. John is just such a person, an agricultural agronomist, an angler, shooting man, cricketer.

Raised in various parts of Africa, John is a true child of the British Empire, not afraid to say what he thinks – so of course we got along. I had seen him around the winter lecture circuit, which we all use to keep ourselves up to speed on new developments. He was always at the seed trial experiments in the summer, his questions were always pertinent and penetrating. That he was very bright no one could doubt. Over lunch we spoke loosely about peas as a viable alternative to oil seed rape. I explained our approach on pigeon control, which led onto rabbit control. Before I left, I gave him an invitation to flight duck with us; I had seen him shoot and knew that his ability was exceptional.

We had a land agent, who dealt with legal things, planning applications and government edicts. We also had consultants dealing with our arable. That particular branch of agriculture was so fast moving, ever on the change, that it had become difficult to keep up with the agro-chemical aspects and fertiliser use. They charged us quite a lot of money for their services without any noticeable benefits in yield. What they also did was treat the soil as nothing more than a growing medium, not the living thing which I knew it to be. They were always taking short cuts, and I didn't wholly trust them. I needed some valid reason to get them gone.

I had discussed it with our land agent who said he too was watching, but I was not to precipitate anything that looked like me breaking our contract with them. My thinking was that John could replace them; it would be cheaper and I for one would feel more comfortable.

First, I had to catch them out for not following the initial brief they were given and signed. Before leaving there were other rituals to go through. Tipping the head keeper, the picker-up, but only if he had done his job properly, then saying goodbye and thanking the host and his wife. The head keeper will be loitering about outside; when you appear, he will hand you a brace of birds and shake your hand, that is when the tip is given. It is very bad form for money to be seen changing hands, your gift will be in the palm of your right hand before you shake hands. I can assure you the keeper will remove it discreetly.

The amount would depend on how well he had done for you. Think about it this way, the wind on this particular day could have spoilt the day; in fact, the head keeper made use of it. Pushing birds away from where they naturally want to fly takes nerves of steel. Then to know by doing it properly and quietly they will curl back over the guns is a trick quite often discussed but seldom actually seen to be done. Today was a master class in the technique, worth an extra five pounds easily. Don't be niggardly, but don't be flash.

The day before the shoot you would have had flowers delivered to your host's wife; she has after all the responsibility of feeding you and several others. Don't do the flowers on shoot day: she will have enough to think about without dealing with fripperies. They love to arrange them, taking time to show the flowers to best effect. Sometimes when you are very hungry after a day's work this flower arranging can try your patience, but when you see the end result you know the wait was worth it.

Driving home the sun was well down and it began to rain, not much, certainly not enough; the screen went smeary with this mud. By the time the Land Rover reached the Winchester bypass, it was raining heavily, and the vehicle has much the same aerodynamics as a bus battered through it, leaving a vortex of spray for the car following. It was with some satisfaction that I saw the top lane of the farm awash with running water.

When you have had a day's shooting by invitation, at the day's end you are handed a brace of whatever birds you were shooting. In the back of the vehicle there were six brace of partridges; five brace I had purchased. They would make something of a feast for everyone. Having spent years trying to increase their own headage of grey partridges, the family decided that, the following year, the farm would import two or three hundred young ones. Not to shoot, but to encourage, with the help of the head keeper next door and the Game Conservancy at Fordingbridge, a stronger indigenous population.

We had obviously been doing something wrong, because over the past five years what had been about two hundred partridges had dropped to about one quarter of this number. The vermin were kept ruthlessly in check. There had not been a magpie or crow nesting on the farm in years, probably not since the war. Foxes, cats, domestic or feral, were given no quarter, everything legal was used against them.

Kestrels would sometimes take the chicks, but not to the detriment of the whole, so that kestrels were spared mainly. The sparrow hawks, however, were a different story. The estate next door used to employ ride-nets*[53] up until the protection of the species became law. These nets are very efficient at catching hawks; the problem is they are not discriminating. If a hawk was chasing, say, a thrush along a ride, both the thrush and the hawk would be enmeshed. The thrush would probably die from being caught, whereas the sparrow hawk would tangle in the net so badly, its neck would have to be pulled to get it out. This all sounds brutally callous, but if the RSPB would publish the real data on how many birds die by sparrow hawks killing them, you would perhaps understand the countryman's attitude to them.

Let me say again, we do not preserve game birds for shooting; we have seen the numbers of grey partridge going down despite our best efforts, so we need to do something. The hares on the farm show that fox, otter and badger predation are not a problem. We do not have many hedgehogs to take the eggs of ground-nesting birds. We have plenty of skylarks, meadow pipits and peewits, so not all of the ground-nesting birds are in decline here. It is a puzzle, which we will find the answer to.

CHAPTER ELEVEN
(November)

November, the real beginning of winter and the need arises to fill the wood store. The Forestry Commission bring in two loads of 'cord wood' in March, forty tons of oak, cut branches from felled trees. Dumped at the sawmill, it is cut to logs for the cottages; for our home the cord is just cut in half. This leaves us with branch wood of varying thickness just over two feet long. When cars became the mode of transport, when horse and traps died out, a garage was built onto the lower part of the house. This became the wood store, dry and connected to the downstairs. The cars have since then been garaged in one of the cart sheds.

With a tractor and trailer, I filled the wood store over a period of about ten days, whenever the rain stopped the arable work. With the cord wood came various 'ugly'*[54] logs, forks so twisted so as to be impossible to split. Some were as much as I could carry. They were generally of various woods, ash, beech, alder or even fruit-wood. These formed the underneath of the fire; the hearth would take two or three of this sort of log, once the fire had some bottom. These big logs would burn and smoulder for perhaps two weeks each. This way the large open fires in the hall could be left to just 'tick over' when heat was not required. Give the logs a good poke, cover them with dry cord wood and soon enough there would be a blaze that threw its warmth out into the great draughty hall.

The house did not have central heating, which in itself was a great blessing; it would have surely driven the farm to bankruptcy else. The Aga heated four radiators, great big cast-iron monsters, the same as generally went into schools. Two-inch cast-iron pipes, through which was pumped hot water, were controlled by a switch on the wall next to the Aga. Every time anybody mentioned having central heating the cry was: 'Why? We will move into the Vicarage shortly.' This had been going on since before the war. (Choose whatever war you want, it makes no difference, the radiators could have been made in the same era as the Dreadnoughts.)

Three stable girls living with us found the house very cold, always going to bed with hot water bottles, despite their beds having electric blankets. In the evenings they would sit in the hearth of the hall fireplace on cushions, toasting themselves like marshmallows. On some evenings they would lie down in a heap on the huge sofa, like puppies in a whelping box and get me to read to them. The current book is *Kon-Tiki*, crossing the Pacific on a balsa-wood raft. If I was too tired for this, one of them would read *A Tale of Two Horses*, taking turns. Their whole lives were completely dedicated to the equine race.

Their daytime routine had changed with the season. Their charges they had brought on over the summer, were now going out on show in the hunting field, to be sold. The younger horses, those destined for eventing, were introduced to hunting. Then going out solo to Wylie to be brought on slowly; again these would sell. There were always around eight hirelings to keep money coming into the business. They were quality animals, which were out most weeks; it was a busy yard. The yearling heifers from last year's calf crop were brought back in now and housed in the open-fronted sheds in the second yard. At this stage they were mixed, Shorthorns and Ayrshires together; the heifers due to have their first calves now were brought into the yards adjacent to their own breed.

That is to say, the Shorthorn first calvers went to a yard next to their older sisters, parent, aunties. There was one common feeding trough running the length of both yards. Their sugar beet was fed to them here. That way the young animals were introduced to their older companions. This always made for easy introduction into the main herd, as it cut down on the bullying from the older animals.

The Ayrshires were the same, except the Ayrshires would fight amongst themselves for a pastime. There were some fairly gruesome and expensive injuries until the herd was 'polled'*[55] by using a naturally polled bull, generally bred up from a breed named Red Poll.

As far as the bull calves that were born this autumn, they were staying with us. Bull calves were being exported to the Continent to be grown on for veal. Thousands were being shipped out; Friesian-Hereford cross calves and pure Friesians were making lots of money in the markets, pure bred Shorthorns were not, which was galling in one way, because Shorthorns were good converters of food and fattened quicker than Friesians. In another way it was a blessing; having been over and seen these veal units in France and Belgium, we had no wish to inflict this on our animals.

We did this year take the opportunity to start a beef unit ourselves; if the country's beef calves were being exported, beef would be short, proper grass-fed beef that is. The Ayrshire bull calves, because the breed was not fit for beef, were sold early to a firm that made baby food. This I found very sad. We obviously kept some for breeding and upgrading the herd, but no more than three or four a year, and at least two of these beasts would be slaughtered before they were two years old, not having made the exacting standards required for breeding. It was heartbreaking to accept that the Ayrshire breed had had its day; exported from Britain to more countries of the world than any other breed, they were now in a steep decline.

When we moved to Devon, there was a herd of Ayrshires near Wincanton; always we slowed down when passing them grazing in their fields, just to look at something different – different from 'These bloody great ugly Friesians' as my aunt always called them.

It seemed nobody in the family wanted to make the decision that the Ayrshires should be replaced. That would mean the original decision to have a second dairy herd, made up of Ayrshires, was a mistake. That would never do. They were not a long-established herd; unlike the Shorthorns, they were brought in because they were a lighter breed and would give us less problems in the foot department. They were also reputed to convert forage better than any other breed, based on the progeny of two very famous Ayrshire herds. I found them very pretty animals, uncomfortable to live with and just as subject to Foul of Foot as any other breed. It had been decreed that over Christmas a decision would be made about the Ayrshires; I thought that would be unlikely.

If ever you feel that you are maybe a failure, plant two long rows of main crop potatoes, follow what the book says, then in due time you have to lift the crop, that is, dig them up. Then you will see that you are not a failure. There is something wonderful about planting one potato, which when you dig it up has multiplied to somewhere between fifteen to twenty potatoes. But not everybody views the kitchen garden in the same light as the gardener, my aunt and myself. When volunteers were called for to perhaps hoe the broad beans, or earth up the potatoes, everybody was busy, too busy to do any gardening.

Detail the farm staff to plant sixty acres of early potatoes, it was done willingly and well. Ask any of the stable girls to load a trailer with dung, it was again done willingly, as long as it was not going to the kitchen garden. Maybe it was because the kitchen garden was walled and gave them a shut-in feeling, but this did not hold good when there were strawberries to gather, or a surfeit of melons growing in the greenhouse, so many that the gardener would surely not miss one. Often was the time in August, when wandering into the stables, the perfume of freshly cut and eaten melon filled the place.

This was Saturday. I had been detailed to work in the kitchen garden, digging potatoes. The river looked clear, beautiful and was running full. Even from the Land Rover – I had parked on the bridge – I could see the grayling rising and falling in the clear water. They looked fit and strong, grabbing at anything that flew past them in the fierce current. One fish was huge, past three pounds, which is a very big grayling. He danced in the current, up and down, eight feet below the surface one second, then taking a morsel of food with a showy splash of his tail from the top. His great dorsal fin red spotted; his flanks showed iridescent green as he dived for the bottom again. I could have lingered and watched them for an hour, but the potatoes demanded I attend them. The 'haulm'[*56] had been removed about ten days ago, now all that showed above the ground, along the ridges, were some dried brown stems. I remained in the garden for about five hours, digging the beautiful pale ruby tubers. The variety was Desiree, a wonderful potato, good for all ways of cooking and looked after properly a very heavy cropper; last year the gardener won the 'main crop potato' class at the town horticultural show. I had helped plant this crop at the back end of March last spring. The garden only had some kale in it, so we could use a small tractor to do the heavy work.

The drills were pulled out with a Ferguson Ridger, grass mowings from the back lawn were laid along the bottom, then the seed potatoes laid on this, 'rose end up'[*57]. The grass mowings were there to prevent scab, a skin disease of potatoes. We never had scab, so I must assume that the idea works. When all the potatoes were sown, that area of the garden looked like a series of fairly high ridges. The next job was to fill the 'valleys' below the ridges with muck; for this we robbed the stable yard muck heap – horse manure is a 'warm' manure and would heat gently as it rotted down.

The benefit of this manure was enormous in yield and quality; in a dry year like we had had, the manure acted as a mulch, keeping the earth damp. At the end of my digging stint, of five hours, I went in for lunch. The pale ruby tubers I left drying in the weak sun; it would strengthen their skins and as a consequence would store better. With perhaps an half an hour of full daylight left of the day's ration, I went back to put the dry potatoes in sacks; about a third of them were gone, the only clue was some tyre marks on the damp exit of the kitchen garden. They were barely the type of tyre that our friends from the trailer park had fitted. These were 'low profile' performance tyres with V-type tread. Where the driver thought he was going I didn't know, he was heading down the west side of the river on a very much single-track lane.

Eventually, I caught up with the car, a Mercedes station wagon, stuck in the mud of the estuary. The lane had been shut off some years before to stop fly-tipping, so consequently the surface had fallen into disrepair. The Mercedes was nose down in a bog. My potatoes were stacked next to it, I suppose in the vain hope of lightening the vehicle to get it unstuck. With the potatoes loaded in the Land Rover I backed for some distance to where I knew an old building had been; turning here I drove back to the kitchen garden. I was sick of these people who thought they had every right to help themselves to what they found while trespassing on our land. There was nothing for me to do but wait now, so I finished bagging and loading what potatoes were left on the ground, then went back to the home yard.

The police were not interested in the theft of the potatoes or the car, which by now should be under four feet of water; high tide and the sluices open at Testwood would make that a certainty. The police were busy with the usual riot that a football match between Southampton and Portsmouth brought about;

such is urban living.

Teatime, the horses were content for the moment, the stable girls sitting down to tea – fresh cooked teacakes, courtesy of Charlotte. The girls looked smart and well groomed; now the evenings were shorter their routine had changed. A rota on doing the evening feed allowed two of them freedom to go out to the cinema and such things. All three of them could go if they persuaded me to do their feeding for them.

Mrs James and Naomi arrived at about six. Lesley showed them into the kitchen. Mrs James was obviously very embarrassed. There was no way out of it for her, I even felt quite sorry for her. It was her husband and brother-in-law who had stolen the potatoes. Naomi had shouted a happy 'Good morning' to me, when she rode past the kitchen garden that morning. She had permission, as long as she was accompanied, by an adult to ride over the farm. Mrs James explained that she had seen the beautiful vegetables, especially the freshly dug potatoes. At home, she had told her husband, saying they should take lessons in growing vegetables, but her husband thought, along with his brother, they wouldn't take lessons. They would rather just take the vegetables. Now their car was stuck in the river mud, her husband's company car. How were they to get it out?

They had not grasped the full seriousness of their situation; loading them into the Land Rover, Jane drove them down to the estuary bridge. With the rabbiting search-light, I showed them their problem. All that was visible was the car's roof, the rest was under muddy water. Naomi began to cry; she had left her hunting cap in the car, a present from her grandmother. Mrs James was very upset; her husband, who was in truth something of a loud-mouthed ne'er do well, had sent her to sort out the problem. I gave her the farm's telephone number and asked that her husband's employers get in touch. Naomi began to cry again, asking if she would still be allowed to ride over the farm. Charlotte said we didn't visit the sins of fathers upon children, then took her out to the stables to show her the horses. And still only half of the potatoes had been dug.

It was obvious that we needed a stricter policy on cars coming onto the place; we decided that any car coming onto the farm had to be disinfected in the interests of disease control. Anybody not wanting their vehicle smelling of Jeyes Fluid would be advised to leave them, in the case of the house, down on the road outside the front gate. Those heading to the farm should leave them in the lane and walk from there.

Pheasant shooting was well under way now; next door was now operating as a commercial shoot, but it wasn't going to last, just an experiment. The keepers 'dogged off'*[58] our land every day, around midday, pushing their pheasants home to stop them wandering too far. The kale was always full of them; why they didn't line the guns out between the kale and their own woods I don't know, except that the pheasants may have seemed too low.

My grandfather and I had invitations to shoot all through the season. Grandfather took them up mainly; pheasant shooting was not a great pleasure to me. In exchange for these invitations we invited people back to flight the duck coming up from the estuary. This I did enjoy; duck is a very sporting quarry, difficult to shoot. Through Barry in the gun shop, we did let an evening to four guns. The shooting is not done by numbers, rather by the light available; by timing the start with the tide coming in we avoided any slaughter of large numbers. Waders were not to be shot, nor yet the peewits; everybody seemed to enjoy 'the day we let some duck shooting', but we never did it again.

Later that same season, we were asked again to allow the same four guns for an evening flight; we voted on it and the answer was a 'no'. We had all felt guilty after the first time, as though we had violated an unwritten law; our wonderful bird life was worth more than money. We shot them sure enough, but for the family to eat, along with the men who worked on the farm – if they wanted to shoot a brace for their family, it was never refused.

On Boxing Day we did have a proper shoot on the duck ponds, for family and friends; our vets were always there and a few close friends. The duck shot were either frozen down for the summer, or given to the old folk, oven ready. Christmas used to be a great get-together on the farm. There were many more people in those days, and it was certainly a lot closer a community. Long before Christmas fifty young cock birds were bought for fattening in one of the open-fronted sheds. When they were six to eight weeks, or when they started fighting amongst themselves, whichever was the sooner, they had to be caponised, gelded in fact.
Capons are cock birds which have been medically castrated. A tiny pellet is injected under their skin on the back of their heads. Two weeks later they begin to behave very oddly. They walk about like Great Bustards, slow, stately and looking very majestic. We used Light Sussex, which grew at a prodigious rate on Blue Cross Sow and Weaner meal, mixed with calf milk powder, then mixed with any skimmed milk available from the dairies into a thick porridge.

They grew into huge birds and because they were never crowded, they stayed on their feet. They never outgrew their strength. On sunny days they were let out onto the nearest grass to have a pick about. They were not in the least flighty. They used to walk about like members of the General Synod, grave, thoughtful and slowly. They never crowed, the injection saw to that, and their combs and wattles never grew; some of the dressed out weights (oven ready) reached sixteen pounds.

These birds were given to our own farm families, along with

ham or beef. These days it is not done, 'too patronising' if you can believe that. The old people, who still lived in their tied cottages, still had them, along with enough coal and wood to carry them through the winter. That is how we said our 'thank you' to the people who worked the farm, or who had worked on the farm, but the younger people didn't really like it.

Harold Wilson's poison had infected everything it touched, not for the better, nor yet for the betterment of older people.

CHAPTER TWELVE
(December)

It was the white flare of car headlights that woke us. Charlotte cuddled close for warmth, mumbled a car had come into the house yard. Half past two in the morning that could only mean trouble; we knew it was the family car, the whine of the pre-selector gearbox told that much. Slipping from the bed gently so as not to allow any cold air in under the covers, I went to the window. The long shape of the Armstrong showed black in the security lights; only one person got out, his aunt. This was trouble. Going downstairs we met in the passageway by the kitchen. 'Hello darling,' she croaked, 'Tea, please.' She was at least smiling. Auntie Niney was the mainstay of my life, tall, beautiful, cool, and forthright.

'Jack is not coming home, my love,' she sighed, holding me close. 'He has taken up with the Keith daughter; your grandfather is even now trying to get him to change his mind. I don't want him now, but the river does.' Niney looked at me with her great deep blue eyes, shielded by lashes so long and black I was convinced they caused their own weather patterns.

Charlotte crept around the door and into the kitchen; she was wearing a heavy brown dressing gown, woollen with a wide belt. For a moment I smiled – Charlotte looked a lot like Badger in *The Wind in the Willows*. 'Has something happened?' she asked shyly, not used to the status of being my fiancée.
'Jack has taken up with another woman, about the same age as you, my dear,' Niney answered.
'Oh dear,' Charlotte said quietly. 'Are you upset?'
'Not really,' Niney answered philosophically, 'if that's what he wants. She has a lovely way with her, don't you think, darling?'

'She is downright ugly, Charlie,' I said. 'She has thick ankles and more than that she is a vegan and farts like a stud horse, and it must be a day's camel march across her backside!'

Charlotte took my hand. 'I'm certain that is not what your aunt wishes to hear.'

Niney snatched her hand up. 'Ooooh! And what is this, Charlotte? Who has been buying you diamonds? Big diamonds, set in white gold, is that?' Charlotte flicked her eyes at me.

'Your nephew asked me to marry him, Niney.'

'Now everything is right again! I'm home, and you two are to be wed. That is wonderful. I wondered who would win, the chestnut filly or the bright bay.' Niney laughed aloud. 'Has he plucked your rose yet?'

Charlotte, who just a few weeks ago had been the essence of purity, now flushed up red, turning her head away.

'Well, that's good my dear ... is he treating you properly? You know what I mean ... no, you probably don't ... we'll talk about it later.' Niney's eyes sparkled with amusement and satisfaction.

Sunday is not really the day for harvesting potatoes, but the forecast was bad, frost by the middle of the week. It would be best to get them up and bagged or stored. This time I was long on help. There was only a rood*[59] at the onset, but the actual size of the crop belied this. Earlier in the year after a fairly heavy storm and blow, the gardener and I had gone down to Milford on Sea and loaded the Land Rover trailer with a very large stack of seaweed. They had just barely managed to get it home; the two-wheeled trailer rocked and leant at crazy angles coming around bends. At Brockenhurst they nearly lost it, one wheel lifted off the road; only by flicking the steering wheel over was the load saved.

As I dug and shook the roots out, the girls and Niney gathered them, gently rubbing the excess soil from them before putting them in the old wheat sacks. Back at the house, they spread them on straw bales, packed tight across the floor of a loose box. This loose box was on the end of a row, no windows and cold, dark and cold, but not freezing; that's what they needed. Should it start to freeze as predicted it would be easy enough to keep the air warmer and circulating in the box.

Deciding on lunch at Mortimers in Ower, we did nothing but wash our hands and change into shoes or joddy boots. This close to Christmas the restaurant was not overcrowded. We all had beef because that was the only meal available. We were noisy, laughing about the Mercedes still sinking in the mud. Pubs and restaurants draw to them almost set types; just up the road was The Vine, all chrome and foreign food, good in its way if that's what you want.

Mortimers was the local place to stay and eat if you were hunting or shooting in the area. I am not going to say 'good plain food'. But if you wanted something which you could pronounce as well as eat, in quantities to satisfy, then Mortimers was the place. They had a good cellar, and the food was sourced locally.

At the end of the meal we discovered none of us had any money with us. We could raise two pounds, fifty-four pence between us. We were making arrangements to pay later when a short thick-set man approached the bar and announced that he would pay the bill, because we had kept his family through the war, without asking for anything in return. This man's father had been posted missing when his ship, a grain carrier, went down. He now had a chance to repay something. There followed a long conversation liberally spiked with: 'Oh yes, I remember. What happened to your pretty sister? Is your mother still alive?'

Niney and I thanked the man who stood us our meal; we sent a bottle of wine to his table to emphasise the point, we were grateful to be remembered. Walking to the car everybody was puffing, gasping with the cold; it really wasn't that cold, just not what we had been used to.

The frost on the tarmac of the car park twinkled in the cold light. The Armstrong's bonnet showed white with frost, except the small patch directly above the engine's block, which clung to the tiny patch of warmth still in the engine.

A 'luxury car' is what it says it is. This Armstrong would throw warmth out of its heater in a couple of minutes from starting. The previous one would seem to take miles before there was any degree of comfort. As the warmth flooded back into the car the girls started to laugh and chatter. They were rather children of the central heating age.

A little weary now, together with Lesley we put around the feed for the horses, checking over each one. They were fine. The stables had already taken on their winter-time smell, molasses, biscuit smelling new crop wheat straw and the perfume of this year's hay. There was no last year's hay to give them, which would have been more normal. There was a school of thought that said new crop hay should not be fed until after Christmas. This was something that you took in with your mother's milk; it wasn't something that you didn't question. They never got very much of the new crop. The rest of the forage was made up with chaffed and molassed barley straw; added to this was extra cabbage and carrots shredded by machine.

When we had finished, we walked up to the house together; it was quite a surprise to have Lesley slip her arm through mine. Lesley was a self-confessed lesbian, always beautifully turned out in black jodhpurs with a white or striped man's shirt, with tailored jackets that must have set her parents back not just a lot of money, but a great heap of money. Of the three girls living with us, Lesley was the most beautiful, a dark-haired stunner with wonderful manners, whose presence in a room could not be ignored. She was a head taller than the other two, sharp, bossy and impatient. She treated men as equals, females as also-rans. When one of the young vets tried it on with her, the slap she gave him sounded the length of the stables.

There was no doubt about her sexual predilection; Lesley had had a fling with the head girl from next door, another with Janet, who rented the stables from us to augment her own yard; she was also, Janet that is, my long-term girlfriend. Lesley also preyed on Jane, who 'went along with it anyhow, because she wasn't getting any sex anywhere else and wanted to see what it was like,' a frank admission that had me crying with laughter.

Charlotte was always different. I met her first when I came home on extended leave from the Services. I had been badly injured. She was the scruffiest person I had ever met; Charlotte seemed to live in a large grey pullover, steeped in hay seeds and horse pee, that came down almost to her knees, with under this jodhpurs that had worn through in places and quite frankly she smelled. This was the enigma; she herself was clean to the point of being shiny, her red-gold hair smelled very expensively kept.

When I took over the running of this yard at home for Janet, whilst she dealt with some pressing family matters, I had the opportunity to put a stop to Lesley bullying and teasing Charlotte. In turn, I was accused of favouritism in my dealings with her by the girls from both yards. Charlotte was easily the best horsewomen amongst them all, and because of her skills she got the best horses to bring on. That of course did not suit the others. They were bluntly told that I matched the skill of the rider to the quality of the animals she looked after; it was therefore up to them in the final analysis what they rode.

There was also the question of 'turn out'; all the girls except Lesley were told to smarten up – it was of little use if the horses looked like polished mahogany, if the person on top looked like a sack of potatoes. This went home hard, because they were all vain, but it worked. They all looked beautiful, Charlotte, maybe because of the difference in her dress, looked the most stunning of all.

The last move was to some subtle PR. I instructed them to pass through the town, make some excuse and stop somewhere, Boots, the Bank, it made no odds and then be wonderfully polite to the crowd that would gather. Let the children fuss the horses and have a young man give whoever had dismounted a leg up. Within a month, the local paper featured them on the front page, describing them as the most charming traffic-calming scheme ever! It all worked rather too well; Janet was flooded with young girls wanting jobs with horses, serious offers of help under the B.H.S. banner, and the usual 'nasties' from the anti-hunting, anti-meat, anti-anything miseries the world has allowed itself to become inflicted with.

It may have been that their friends the potato heads were working themselves up for the Boxing Day meets coming up soon. They parked themselves outside the front gates, yelling abuse at anyone they saw. They had been there for about three hours on this particular day. They were not causing me any problems; we had other entrances. It was around lunch-time that a large blue tractor went past them pulling a slurry tanker. Half the potato heads were yelling at it, the others tried to stop it passing. There is a rural expression which covers what happened next.

The potato heads were suddenly in 'a world of shit'.

A slurry tanker is powered from the tractor's power take off; the driver claimed later that this had jumped into gear going over a bump. These machines can throw thick liquid dung for fifty metres or more; the potato heads were absolutely coated in it, as were their cars and vans, and it smelled rather like chicken muck. Not our fault then. We don't have chickens, only the hens that live around the farm buildings, but we were going to be in the firing line for certain.

The slurry caused considerable damage to some of the cars. The tanker's pump must have been flat out, because one jet knocked a woman on her back. The tractor went on down the lane that would eventually lead to Redbridge, going very quickly, spewing out slurry, black diesel smoke from its exhaust and mud from its tyres. To this day I still maintain that I do not know who it was, someone who was fed up to the back teeth with townie people telling us what was what, no doubt.

There was going to be trouble about it for certain: one rather smart Saab had its canvas roof open and had thirty or forty gallons dumped in it; more importantly some of the protesters had inadvertently swallowed bits of the slurry. Several of these people had come from as far afield as Sussex University, but mostly from Southampton or Basingstoke; wherever they came from they were fairly angry. When the police had convinced them that we had had nothing to do with the flying slurry, we filled the water bowser and let them wash themselves down.

The police wanted us to let them wash themselves in one of the yards, but we refused this because the potato heads would surely have taken the opportunity to note down anything they saw that was worth stealing. It was like being under siege – normal decent people seemed not immune from seeing something, ostensibly lying around and then stealing it. Simon from Milk Hill near Marlborough had noted it; in fact it was more prevalent within the new incomers than with our friends from the caravan park.

The Mercedes station wagon down in the estuary had become a write off, removed by a large crane reaching over the fence. The chassis had twisted, or what was called a chassis. It was a company car. The driver received no censure whatever; in fact, the 'transport manager' of the London firm saw the whole thing as amusing, and the insurers had paid.

What hope was there for rural people to be able to live alongside this dross? The transport manager informed me that Wayne, the potato stealer, was on the way to 'the top', a 'very good man'. I remarked that scum had a habit of doing this, rising to 'the top', which seemed lost on the transport manager.

It was going to be a strange sort of Christmas with my grandfather and uncle not being at home. My aunt busied herself with the preparations for it none the less. The girls had all elected to stay over Christmas. Now they were staying in the farmhouse they had settled down to our more domestic pattern. It had its benefits: their food was prepared for them, provided they helped, their washing done for them and despite there being no central heating, they soon got used to the chill in the air in the mornings.

For my part, I thoroughly enjoyed their being there. What bloke wouldn't – three beautiful, lively, leggy females, living cheek by jowl with me? They wandered about in their sleeping gear, filling the air with their exotic scents in the evenings, sitting in the hearth brushing each other's hair, like so many mermaids.

The Christmas Horse Show at Olympia was filling their minds

at the minute, how they were going to divide the workload so that some of them at least could attend. Jane was not that keen on going, so it was decided that myself and she would cope with the horses here at home. The one night they were away, clashed with the NFU Christmas dinner and dance and was also my birthday. My aunt was not attending, so I took Jane, who was something of a star turn on the dance floor.

Janet and her stable girls were coming to us for their Christmas dinner; it was more than strange with no grandfather.

Before the advent of automatic milking, the whole family would split themselves up to go to one of the dairies or the pig unit. This was to help the dairymen and stockman to finish early, so they could spend more time at home on Christmas Day. Nobody was needed these days; the cows fed themselves by computer, the milk was measured and chilled by computer, the parlours washed and dried by computer. Even the slurry was delivered to the designated fields by computer, spreading it about in a thick mist on the spring wheat land. We were still farming the same acres, getting higher yields, but doing less ourselves with less staff. It was very efficient but desperately boring; it got to the stage that unloading some muck in somebody's garden with a dung prong became a novelty.

The horses were still very much 'hands on', and those hunting on Boxing Day would need to be looking their very best, though unless the weather changed there would be no actual hunting. They would still meet at Lyndhurst, but this year it was going to be still too hard and frosty; it was tradition and a social thing. Janet would also hope to sell some horses or at least some buyers would make the first moves towards purchase.

In the event the meet was changed at the last minute, the hunt was going to be targeted by the anti-hunting lunatics; a contingency plan was put into play. The meet was transferred to the Royal Oak: which one, though? Well, we all knew but there were lots of Royal Oaks in the New Forest. Hunt foot followers would still go to The Bench in Lyndhurst, along with people who worked on the forest, farm blokes whose day had been spoiled. They mingled with the tourists who did not know the venue had been changed and were pretty fed up. They were being stirred up by the foot followers more than somewhat. When the antis did arrive carrying banners and clubs, they had a pretty warm reception. The police found themselves defending the antis from the touristy folk. The meet at the Royal Oak had gone off well. They did hunt gently, the ground being not quite so hard over that side of the forest. The police were miffed because they had not been told, but why should they have been? They were on the side of the antis and would doubtless have told them what was to happen.

Anyway, why does anybody think that police are needed at a fox hunt meet? We can look after ourselves and the antis if they turn up.

It had been a quiet and restrained sort of Christmas. The food had been wonderful, but the girls from Janet's yard had been very reserved. They had never been in the 'big house' before. They spoke in whispers amongst themselves, occasionally giggling, sitting together at the far end of the table. Personally, I was glad when it was over; it showed me that we, my aunt, and I, were from a different age. Lesley, Jane, and Charlotte tried to jolly things along, but the other girls became even more reserved.

They, Janet's girls, looked relieved when Janet said it was time to go and they were into their outside clothes very quickly. When quiet had descended again, we sat around looking at each other, rather deflated until Charlotte started to giggle, 'It's the lead water pipes over that side of the valley, turns people into hillbillies.'

It was enough to get them laughing again, even if Niney's laughter was somewhat muted; my aunt knew, as did I, that this was something of a crossroads for us. We didn't really know what was ahead; we did know however, that shortly the rooks would be repairing their nests again, only this morning the mistle thrush was singing from the top of the ash tree.

AND NOW WE END...

So much is unspoken, so much is unwritten about a countryman's year.

I live on an island at the end of the day.

And as more people are born and indeed emigrate to this septred isle, so it can seem as if urban development and the modern way of living, in towns and even gated communities, is creeping inevitably to my farm gate.

In MY lifetime there is a fair chance that this seemingly unstoppable force may not reach the five bars that seperate my green and pleasant land, but for those who come after me to till, grow and harvest this sweet soil, I have no predictions.

THIS was a year - It is my own. My memories of Tinkers, Townies and Toffs.

Time now to load my pipe and trailer. There is always work to be done and each new tree planted and every field tended, helps preserve a way of life that is so very rich in value and content.

May this book play a part in preserving the memory of the countrtman as well.

* * * * *

ABOUT THE AUTHOR

A lifetime spent growing up, living and working in the countryside woven together.

Tinkers, townies and toffs is a tale of a countryman's experiences and observations. The author needed a diversion from his struggles with another title, so what better distraction than the natural world he could observe from his writing desk.

Born during the 2nd world war when food was rationed and agriculture was more highly valued.

Childhood spent in the New Forest with either a catapult or fishing rod in hand.

Worked in farming and dealing of farm supplies and produce.

Started a clay pigeon shooting school in Hampshire.

Moved the family and shooting school to Devon.

Wrote articles for several country sports magazines.
Tried to have country sports defined as a religion to protect them.

Was working on a series of spy novels when he died.

ROD BRAMMER

****

SHALDEN SHOOTING SCHOOL

https://www.shootingschooldevon.co.uk

info@shootingschooldevon.co.uk

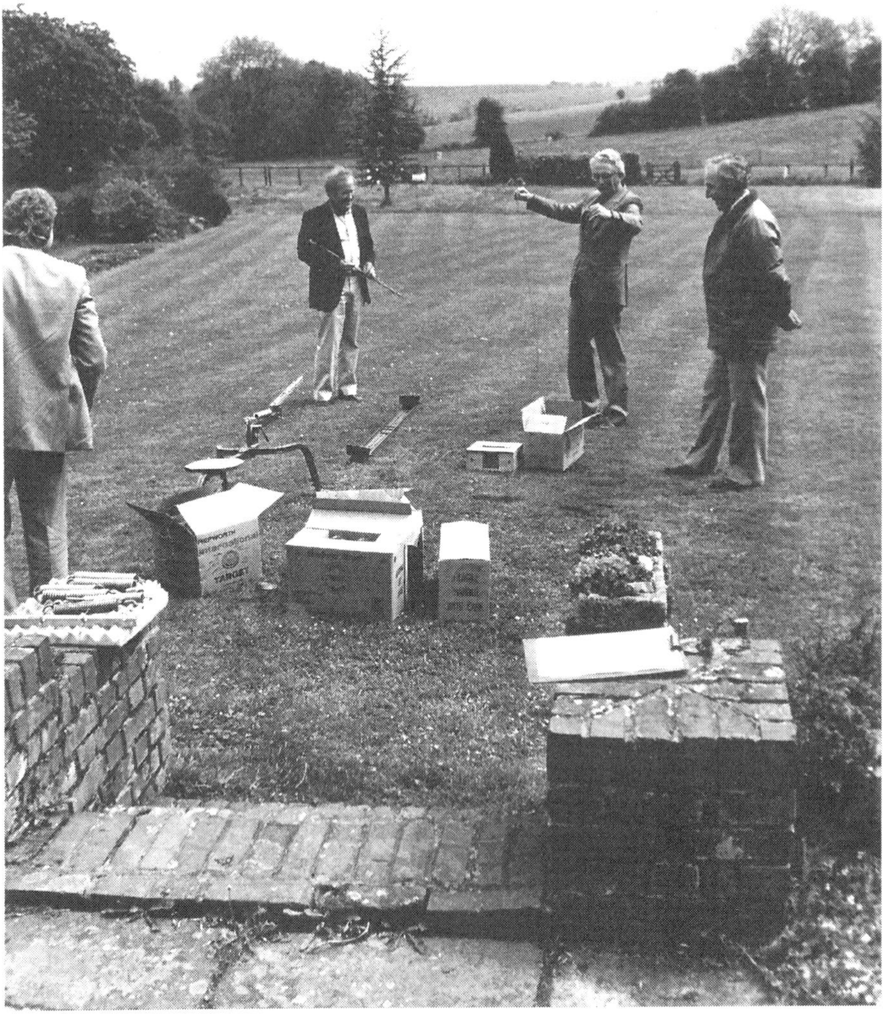
TARGET

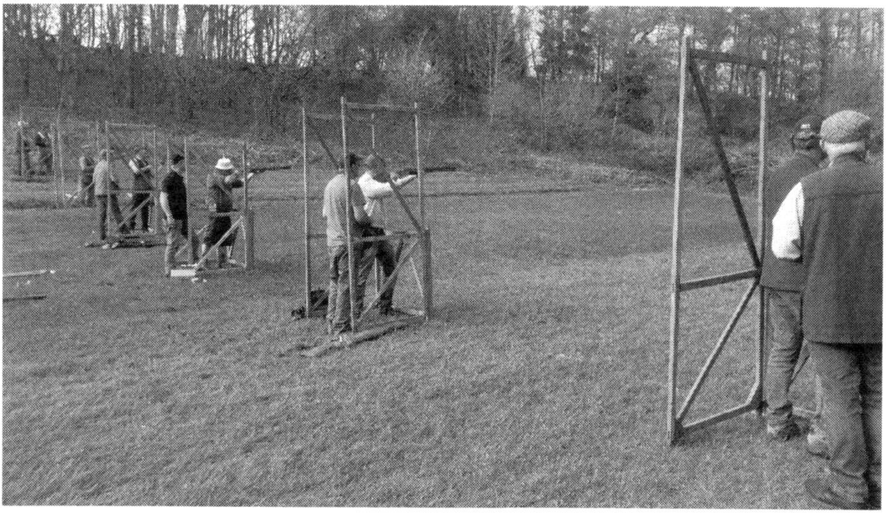

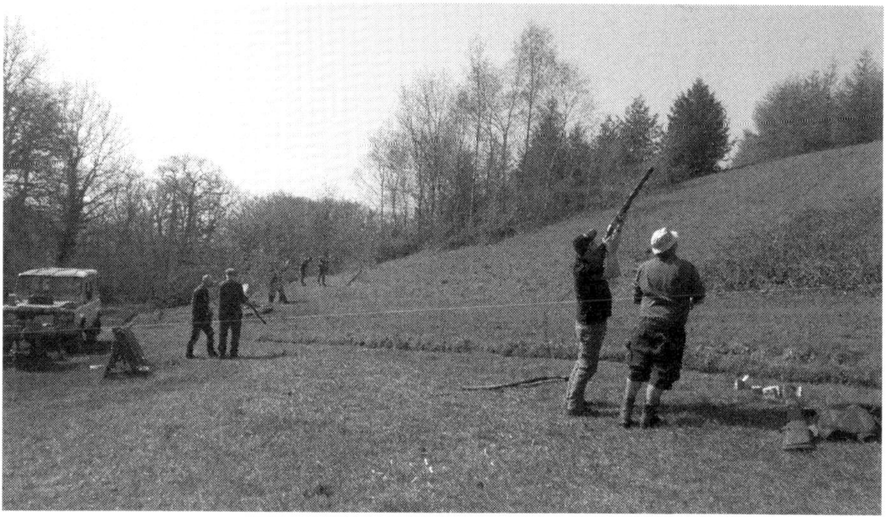

Printed in Great Britain
by Amazon